FREE CAMPGROUNDS

OF WASHINGTON & OREGON

Third Edition

By KiKi Canniff

Ki² Enterprises
P.O. Box 186
Willamina, Oregon 97396

Third Edition
Copyright © 1992
by
KiKi Canniff

No part of this book may be reproduced in any form by any electronic or mechanical means including information storage and retrieval systems, without permission in writing from the publisher. All rights reserved.

Library of Congress Cataloging in Publication Data

Canniff, KiKi
Free Campgrounds of Washington & Oregon / by KiKi Canniff —
Rev. ed.   p.   cm.
Includes indexes.
ISBN 0-941361-04-7 : $8.95
1. Camp sites, facilities, etc. - Washington (State) - Directories. 2. Camp sites, facilities, etc. - Oregon - Directories. I. Title. II. Title: Free Campgrounds of Washington & Oregon.
GV191.42.W2C35   1992   91-44868
647.9479709—dc20   CIP

ISBN 0-941361-04-7

Ki^2 Enterprises
P.O. Box 186
Willamina, Oregon 97396

TABLE OF CONTENTS

Introduction 9
Where to find Oregon's free campgrounds 13-75
    Oregon Map 14
    Agness 15
    Azalea 15
    Baker City 15
    Bandon 15
    Beaver 15
    Bend 16
    Blue River 19
    Bly 19
    Burns 20
    Butte Falls 20
    Camp Sherman 21
    Cascade Locks 22
    Cave Junction 22
    Chemult 22
    Chiloquin 23
    Christmas Valley 23
    Coos Bay 23
    Coquille 24
    Cove 24
    Crescent 24
    Crescent Lake 24
    Culp Creek 25
    Culver 26
    Dale 26
    Detroit 27
    Diamond Lake 27
    Dufur 27
    Elgin 28
    Enterprise 28
    Estacada 29
    Florence 33
    Fort Rock 33
    Fox 33
    Gardiner 34
    Glide 34
    Gold Beach 35
    Government Camp 35
    Haines 37

Halfway	37
Hebo	37
Heppner	38
Hood River	38
Idleyld Park	38
Imnaha	38
Jacksonville	39
John Day	39
Jordan Valley	40
Joseph	40
Kimberly	41
Klamath Falls	41
La Grande	42
Lakeview	42
LaPine	43
Lostine	45
Lowell	46
Marial	46
Maupin	46
McKenzie Bridge	47
Medical Springs	47
Mehama	48
Minam	48
Mitchell	48
Mt. Vernon	49
Myrtle Point	49
Oakridge	49
Oxbow	51
Paisley	52
Parkdale	53
Paulina	54
Pendleton	55
Port Orford	55
Powers	55
Prairie City	56
Prineville	57
Prospect	58
Remote	59
Richland	59
Rogue River	59
Rome	60
Scappoose	60
Selma	60

Seneca 60
Silver Lake 61
Sisters 61
Sixes 62
Spray 63
Steamboat 63
Sumpter 65
Sunriver 66
Taft 66
Tiller 66
Tollgate 68
Tygh Valley 69
Ukiah 70
Union 71
Unity 71
Vale 72
Waldport 72
Wallowa 72
Wamic 73
Westfir 74
Weston 74
White City 74
Whitney 75
Yachats 75
Where to find Washington's free campgrounds 77-126
  Washington Map 78
  Asotin 79
  Barstow 79
  Belfair 79
  Boyds 81
  Burlington 81
  Carson 81
  Castle Rock 82
  Chelan 82
  Chewelah 85
  Cle Elum 85
  Colville 87
  Conconully 88
  Concrete 88
  Cook 90
  Cougar 90
  Coupeville 90
  Curlew 90

Darrington	90
Dayton	91
Elbe	92
Eldon	92
Ellensburg	92
Entiat	93
Enumclaw	94
Forks	94
Fort Spokane	95
Goldendale	96
Grand Coulee	96
Granite Falls	96
Hoodsport	98
Humptulips	98
Hunters	98
Ilwaco	99
Index	99
Ione	100
Kettle Falls	100
Leavenworth	102
Loomis	104
Marblemount	105
Montesano	106
Naches	106
Neah Bay	109
North Bend	109
Okanogan	109
Olympia	110
Orient	111
Packwood	111
Pomeroy	113
Port Angeles	114
Queets	115
Quilcene	115
Randle	115
Republic	117
Riverside	117
San Juan Islands	117
Sequim	119
Spokane	120
Tampico	120
Tonasket	121
Trout Lake	121

Twisp	123
Usk	124
Vancouver	124
Wilbur	125
Wilkeson	125
Winthrop	125
Campground Index	127
General Index	139

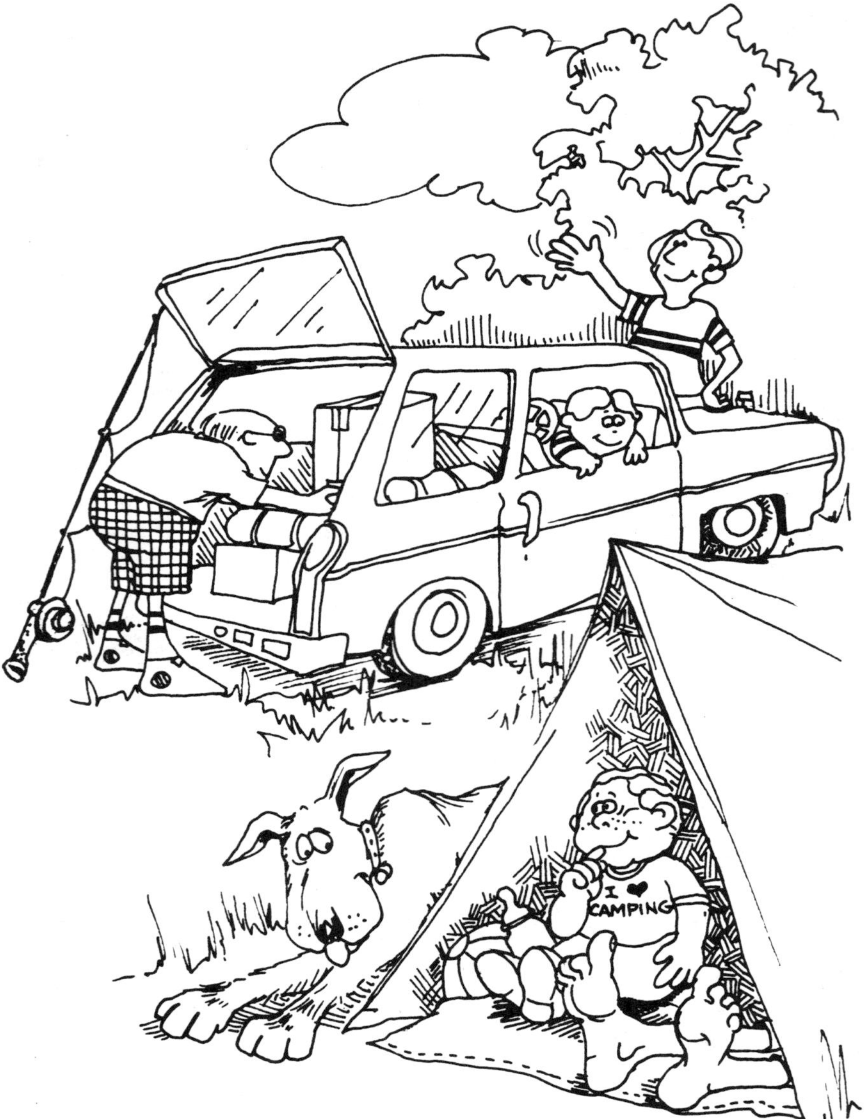
I ♥ CAMPING

INTRODUCTION

Washington and Oregon campgrounds offer outdoor enthusiasts the opportunity to experience a variety of landscapes. You can camp in the woods or a mountain meadow, beside a lazy river or rushing stream or under the stars in the open desert. Rugged canyons, quiet islands, lake shores and wilderness areas can be your home for the night.

Free campgrounds are abundant in this region and can be enjoyed throughout both states. **Free Campgrounds of Washington & Oregon** was written to help camping enthusiasts experience the natural side of camping; staying where all but the most basic trappings of civilization have been ignored.

In Oregon's southeastern corner you'll discover part of the famed Great Basin. This is a stark wilderness landscape made up of breathtaking mountains and high desert country. The state's northeastern corner offers mountainous campsites in an area aptly nicknamed "Little Switzerland". It holds 126 mountain peaks, all between 8,000 and 10,000 feet high, 11 glacially carved canyons and more than 150 alpine lakes. Many consider Oregon's Wallowa Mountains the state's most spectacular region.

Central Oregon campers will find a beautiful desert, the continental United States' largest collection of volcanic remains, crisp mountain air and a backdrop of snow covered mountains. The Cascade Mountains, which divide both states, are dotted with campgrounds from border to border.

Although you'll find fewer free campgrounds west of the I-5 corridor and along the coast, quite a few do exist. However, these are often filled up by late afternoon so plan on stopping early.

In western Washington you can camp in a rain forest. Giant moss-draped spruce trees 300' tall and the largest variety of wild mushrooms in the continental United States can be found near Forks. You can also visit the Olympic National Park which protects America's last wilderness beach.

Some of the smaller San Juan Islands, northwest of Seattle, are covered entirely by public parks. These offer boaters isolated campsites where lush greenery is surrounded by sparkling blue water. Northeast of Seattle you'll find a wealth of campsites for land bound enthusiasts along with Bald Eagle nesting areas, ice caves, the spectacular Cascade Loop, wild and scenic rivers and lots of hiking trails. This state's portion of the Cascade Mountain Range is dotted with free campsites too.

Washington's northeastern corner is a haven for those who love the outdoors. Caves, ghost towns, fishing, historic sites and hiking trails provide lots of activities. The state's southeastern corner was once winter camp to the Nez Perce Indians and is as appealing to campers today as it must have been to the Nez Perce for centuries past.

Whether you choose to sleep beneath the stars, in a tent or in the comfort of a recreational vehicle, this book will help you find the right spot. Camping restores the spirit. Cares seem to evaporate on the wind when exposed to the fresh air, open spaces and gentle sounds of nature. Coping with near primitive conditions also brings a feeling of self-reliance. Children gain a knowledge of conservation and a love for wildlife and the land it calls home.

Throughout this two state region, campgrounds located near sea level open earlier (April) and remain open later (November) than those found at higher elevations. Spring arrives late in the mountains and with it a carpet of wildflowers. Blueberries, blackberries, strawberries, rose hips, wild vegetables and mushrooms are abundant in many northwest areas later in the year.

Most of the campgrounds listed in this book have picnic tables, fire rings and toilet facilities. Many exist in less trampled areas where you will find easy access to spectacular scenery, hiking trails, fishing and a chance to enjoy nature.

Free campgrounds generally receive less maintenance than other campgrounds. Only as long as each visitor leaves a clean camp, taking their garbage out with them, can we be assured these campgrounds will remain open. Do not throw garbage down outhouse holes or future campers will soon be without facilities.

When toilet facilities are not available, body wastes should be treated in much the same way a cat uses sand. Dig a shallow hole (6" is plenty deep) and cover your waste, including toilet paper, with dirt. Stomp the dirt down firmly.

If piped or well water is not available you should boil lake water for at least 5 minutes before consuming. Many campers consider streams that rush over 30' or more of rocks and sand to be clean enough to drink. When in doubt boil or add Halazone tables.

Campfires should be built in fire rings whenever possible. If no fire ring is available select an area away from brush and overhanging branches and clear the land down to mineral soil. When breaking camp, all fires should be stirred up and sprinkled heavily with water. If you hesitate to stick your hand into last night's ashes, it's not out well enough to leave.

This book was designed to be used together with your state highway map. Each state's tourism office gives these away free. The maps provided in this book will help you to locate the general area you plan to visit. The map's grid coordinates are also printed beside each city's listing to help you to find other cities within the area you plan to visit.

Campgrounds are listed alphabetically by city. Each individual listing begins with the campground name followed by that of its operating agency. Next, you will find a brief list of facilities. The final information consists of simply stated directions. FSR has been substituted for Forest Service Road and CR for County Road.

For your convenience, an alphabetical listing of all the campgrounds in this book can be found in the campground index at the back of the book. This can be used to quickly find campgrounds you know by name.

A good portion of the campgrounds listed here are operated by the U.S. Forest Service and Bureau of Land Management (BLM). Detailed maps can be obtained from both agencies which clearly show roads, trails, lakes, rivers and streams. You can stop at any area BLM or Forest Service office for a look at their display copy, or for a small charge, you can purchase your own. This will make finding the campground easier and let you know about nearby attractions.

If you are unable to find an available campsite on Forest Service or BLM land you still have one free alternative left. As long as you choose a spot that is at least 100 yards from any body of water or developed campground, and it is not posted otherwise, you can set up camp. If you build a fire, you must use caution when selecting a site and are required to have a shovel and bucket handy. Bury all body wastes, pack out your garbage and return your temporary campsite to its original condition or better and no one will chase you away.

Besides free campgrounds, an additional 1,500 "pay" campgrounds exist in Washington and Oregon. Many offer showers, trailer waste disposal, hookups for water, electricity and sewer plus other amenities associated with civilization. Some even have swimming pools, laundry facilities and cable tv. You will find these campgrounds detailed in **A Camper's Guide to Oregon & Washington** by the same author.

WHERE TO FIND OREGON'S FREE CAMPGROUNDS

OREGON MAP

AGNESS (A-11)

ILLAHE (Siskiyou National Forest)
20 units, trailers to 22', picnic area, piped water, river, flush toilets, fishing, elev. 300'.
Northeast of Agness. CR 375 north 4.9 miles, located along Rogue River.

AZALEA (B-11)

DEVILS FLAT (Umpqua National Forest)
3 units, trailers to 18', picnic facilities, nearby historic cabin, Cow Creek Falls Trail, fishing, hiking, elev. 2200'.
East of Azalea. CR 36 east 17 miles.

BAKER CITY (E-9)

BASSER DIGGINS (BLM)
15 units, water, picnic facilities, hiking, elev. 6800'.
Southeast of Baker City. Located 30 miles southeast of town, northeast of I-84 at Lookout Mountain.

BANDON (A-11)

BRADLEY LAKE BOAT RAMP (Coos County)
Camping area, picnic facilities, pit toilets, boat ramp, fishing, hiking.
South of Bandon. US Highway 101 south 3.7 miles, Bradley Lake Road west to boat ramp area.

BEAVER (A-8)

ALDER GLEN (BLM)
11 units, drinking water, swimming, elev. 700'.
East of Beaver. Nestucca Road east 18.0 miles.

DOVRE (BLM)
12 units, drinking water, swimming, elev. 1500'.
East of Beaver. Nestucca Road 21.0 miles east.

ELK BEND (BLM)
3 units, drinking water, year round, elev. 950'.
East of Beaver. Nestucca Road 20.0 miles east.

FAN CREEK (BLM)
12 units, drinking water, swimming, elev. 1300'.
East of Beaver. Nestucca Road 24.0 miles east.

BEND (D-10)

BIG RIVER (Deschutes National Forest)
13 units, trailers to 22', on Deschutes River, boating, fishing, elev. 4200'.
Southwest of Bend. US Highway 97 south 22.0 miles, CR 42 southwest 5.0 miles.

DEVILS LAKE (Deschutes National Forest)
6 units, trailers to 22', lake - no motors, boating, swimming, fishing, elev. 5500'.
West of Bend. State Highway 46 west 20.0 miles, CR 46 west 6.0 miles.

DILLON FALLS (Deschutes National Forest)
5 units, trailers to 32', on Deschutes River, boating, fishing, elev. 4000'.
West of Bend. State Highway 46 west 6.5 miles, FSR 41 southwest 2.3 miles then .9 mile southeast.

IRISH & TAYLOR (Deschutes National Forest)
12 tent units, lake - no motors, boating, fishing, trails, rough road, no tables, elev. 5700'.
Southwest of Bend. State Highway 46 west 20.0 miles, CR 46 southwest 23.6 miles, FSR 4630 southwest 3.0 miles, FSR 600 west 5.0 miles.

LITTLE CULTUS (Deschutes National Forest)
12 units, trailers to 22', well, lake - speed limit, boating, fishing, swimming, hiking, elev. 4800'.
Southwest of Bend. State Highway 46 west 20.0 miles, CR 46 southwest 23.6 miles, FSR 4630 southwest 3.0 miles, FSR 600 west 1.0 mile.

LITTLE LAVA LAKE (Deschutes National Forest)
14 units, trailers to 22', lake - speed limits, fishing, boating, elev. 4800'.
Southwest of Bend. State Highway 46 west 20.0 miles, CR 46 southwest 14.0 miles, FSR 500 northeast .5 mile.

MALLARD MARSH (Deschutes National Forest)
15 units, trailers to 22', well, on Hosmer lake - speed limit, fishing, elev. 4900'.
Southwest of Bend. State Highway 46 west 20.0 miles, CR 46 southwest 11.3 miles, FSR 4625 southeast 2.7 miles.

MCKAY CROSSING (Deschutes National Forest)
10 units, trailers to 22', stream, fishing, elev. 4400'.
Southeast of Bend. US Highway 97 south 22.0 miles, CR 21 east 5.0 miles, FSR 9736 north 1.2 miles.

MILE (Deschutes National Forest)
8 units, trailers to 22', on Upper Deschutes River, fishing, elev. 4700'.
Southwest of Bend. State Highway 46 west 20.0 miles, CR 46 southeast 16.0 miles, just off highway.

NORTH TWIN LAKE (Deschutes National Forest)
12 units, trailers to 22', lake - no motors, fishing, swimming, elev. 4300'.
Southwest of Bend. State Highway 46 west 20.0 miles, CR 46 southwest 27.0 miles, FSR 42 for 4.0 miles to FSR 4260 and campground.

ROSLAND (Deschutes National Forest)
11 units, trailers to 22', picnic area, no drinking water, Little Deschutes River, swimming, fishing, elev. 4200'.
South of Bend. US Highway 97 south 23.0 miles, CR 43 west 2.0 miles.

SAND SPRINGS (Deschutes National Forest)
6 units, trailers to 22', group sites, no water, primitive, elev. 5100'.
Southeast of Bend. US Highway 20 east 20.0 miles, CR 23 southeast 5.0 miles, FSR 23 southeast 13.6 miles to junction with FSR 22 and 2312, turn right on FSR 22 to campground.

SLOUGH (Deschutes National Forest)
4 units, trailers to 18', on Deschutes River, fishing, elev. 4000'.
Southwest of Bend. State Highway 46 southwest 6.5 miles, FSR 41 southwest .5 mile, FSR 4120 south 3.0 miles, FSR 41 southwest .5 mile.

SODA CREEK (Deschutes National Forest)
12 units, trailers to 22', on Sparks Lake - no motors, fishing, elev. 5400'.
Southwest of Bend. State Highway 46 west 20.0 miles, CR 46 southwest 5.2 miles, FSR 400 south .1 mile.

SOUTH (Deschutes National Forest)
23 units, trailers to 22', picnic area, Hosmer Lake - speed limits, boat launch, fishing, elev. 4900'.
Southwest of Bend. State Highway 46 west 20.0 miles, CR 46 southwest 14.0 miles, FSR 4625 southwest 1.0 mile.

SWAMP WELLS HORSE CAMP (Deschutes National Forest)
5 units, trailers to 22', horse camp, elev. 5400'.
Southeast of Bend. US Highway 97 south 1.5 miles, FSR 18 east 6.0 miles, FSR 1810 south 5.5 miles, FSR 1816 southeast 2.2 miles. Campground is centrally located on Trail #61 between Horse Butte & Newberry Crater.

TODD LAKE (Deschutes National Forest)
4 walk-in tent units, picnic area, lake - no motors, very scenic, fishing, boating, elev. 6200'.
West of Bend. State Highway 46 west 20.0 miles, CR 46 southwest 2.0 miles, FSR 370 north .2 mile, hike-in .1 mile to lake.

TUMALO FALLS (Deschutes National Forest)
4 tent units, picnic area, stream, fishing, elev. 5000'.
West of Bend. Galveston Street west 3.0 miles, FSR 4601 west 7.0 miles, FSR 4603 west 2.0 miles. Closed in late summer, watershed for Bend.

WEST CULTUS (Deschutes National Forest)
15 tent units, boat-in or hike-in only, piped water, on Cultus Lake, fishing, swimming, water skiing, elev. 4700'.

Southwest of Bend. State Highway 46 west 20.0 miles, CR 46 southwest 26.5 miles, FSR 4635 northwest 1.5 miles, boat across lake 2.7 miles or take Trail #16 for 3.2 miles.

BLUE RIVER (C-10)

BOX CANYON HORSE CAMP (Willamette National Forest)
14 units, trailers to 22', stream, trails, elev. 3700'.
Southeast of Blue River. State Highway 126 east 3.5 miles, FSR 19 south 27.0 miles around reservoir to campground.

DUTCH OVEN (Willamette National Forest)
4 units, river, fishing, primitive, elev. 2100'.
Southeast of Blue River. State Highway 126 east 3.5 miles, FSR 19 south 22.0 miles around reservoir to campground.

HOMESTEAD (Willamette National Forest)
7 units, river, fishing, primitive, elev. 2200'.
Southeast of Blue River. State Highway 126 east 3.5 miles, FSR 19 south 23.5 miles around reservoir to campground.

TWIN SPRINGS (Willamette National Forest)
5 units, trailers okay, river, fishing, elev. 2400'.
Southeast of Blue River. State Highway 126 east 3.5 miles, FSR 19 south 25.5 miles around reservoir to campground.

BLY (D-12)

CORRAL CREEK (Fremont National Forest)
5 units, no well, fishing, remote, elev. 5900'.
Northeast of Bly. State Highway 140 east 1.0 miles, FSR 34 northeast 17.0 miles to campground.

LOFTON RESERVOIR (Fremont National Forest)
17 units, trailers to 30', well, lake - electric motors only, boating, good fishing, elev. 6200'.
Southeast of Bly. State Highway 140 southeast 12.9 miles, FSR 3715 south 7.0 miles, FSR 3715013 northeast 1.3 miles.

BURNS (E-10)

IDLEWILD (Malheur National Forest)
24 units, trailers to 32', picnic area, piped water, elev. 5300'.
North of Burns. US Highway 395 north 17.0 miles.

ROCK SPRINGS (Malheur National Forest)
8 units, trailers to 22', piped water, elev. 5000'.
North of Burns. US Highway 395 north 33.8 miles, FSR 17 east 4.5 miles, FSR 054 southeast 1.0 miles.

ROME (BLM)
Campsites, water, restrooms, picnic facilities, boat ramp.
East of Burns. Located on the Owyhee River, 13 miles east of Burns Junction.

YELLOWJACKET (Malheur National Forest)
20 units, trailers to 22', piped water, lake - speed limits, boat launch, boating, swimming, fishing, elev. 4800'.
Northwest of Burns. US Highway 20 south 1.0 mile, FSR 47 northwest 32.0 miles, FSR 37 east 4.0 miles, FSR 3745 south .5 mile.

BUTTE FALLS (C-11)

BIG BEN (Rogue River National Forest)
2 tent units, stream, fishing, hiking, elev. 4000'.
Northeast of Butte Falls. Take CR 30 southeast 14.1 miles, FSR 34 northeast 8.2 miles, FSR 37 southeast .8 mile.

IMNAHA (Rogue River National Forest)
4 tent units, stream, fishing, remote, elev. 3800'.
Northeast of Butte Falls. Take CR 30 southeast 2.7 miles, FSR 37 northeast 8.0 miles.

SNOWSHOE (Rogue River National Forest)
5 tent units, well, elev. 4000'.
East of Butte Falls. CR 30 southeast 9.3 miles, FSR 3065 northeast 4.8 miles.

SOUTH FORK (Rogue River National Forest)
6 tent units, trailers to 18', stream, fishing, remote, elev. 4000'.
Northeast of Butte Falls. CR 30 southeast 14.1 miles, FSR 34 northeast 7.7 miles.

CAMP SHERMAN (C-9)

ABBOTT CREEK (Deschutes National Forest)
4 units, trailers to 18', fishing, elev. 3100'.
Northwest of Camp Sherman. FSR 14 north 3.0 miles, FSR 1419 northwest 2.0 miles to junction of FSR 1420, north 5.0 miles.

CANDLE CREEK (Deschutes National Forest)
5 units, trailers to 18', stream, fishing, elev. 2800'.
North of Camp Sherman. FSR 14 north 7.0 miles, FSR 980 north 1.5 miles.

JACK CREEK (Deschutes National Forest)
11 units, 5 group sites, trailers to 16', stream, fishing, elev. 3100'.
Northwest of Camp Sherman. State Highway 20 to FSR 12, northwest 4.5 miles to FSR 1230, go .2 mile north to campground.

JACK LAKE (Deschutes National Forest)
2 units, lake - no motors, boating, swimming, fishing, horse facilities, trailhead into Mt. Jefferson Wilderness, elev. 5100'.
Northwest of Camp Sherman. State Highway 20 to FSR 12, northwest 4.5 miles to FSR 1230, follow for 1.0 mile to FSR 1234 then go 4.0 miles to campground on Jack Lake.

LOWER CANYON CREEK (Deschutes National Forest)
5 units, trailers to 18', fishing, trails, elev. 2900'.
North of Camp Sherman. FSR 14 north 3.0 miles, FSR 1419 northwest 2.0 miles, FSR 1420 3.0 miles, FSR 400 .5 mile to campground.

RIVERSIDE (Deschutes National Forest)
22 units, trailers ok, group sites, well, stream, elev. 3000'.

South of Camp Sherman. FSR 14 south 2.0 miles, located 2.0 miles south of Camp Sherman Store.

CASCADE LOCKS (C-7)

HERMAN CREEK CAMP (Mt. Hood National Forest)
7 units, trailers to 32', picnic area, wheelchair access, boat launch, boating, swimming, fishing, water skiing, hiking, horse trails - corrals - hitch posts, bicycling, elev. 200'.
East of Cascade Locks. Take County Road east 1.6 miles.

SEVEN & ONE-HALF MILE (Mt. Hood National Forest)
15 tent units, hike-in only, not maintained, shelter, stream, fishing, elev. 1500'.
West of Cascade Locks. I-84 west 4.5 miles, I-84 east 2.0 miles, FSR 240 southeast .1 mile to Eagle Creek Campground, Eagle Creek Trail 4.5 miles to campground.

WY'EAST (Mt. Hood National Forest)
5 tent units, hike-in only, not maintained, shelter, stream, fishing, elev. 1200'.
West of Cascade Locks. I-84 west 4.5 miles, I-84 east 2.0 miles, FSR 240 southeast .1 mile to Eagle Creek Campground, Eagle Creek Trail 4.6 miles to campground.

CAVE JUNCTION (A-12)

BOLAN LAKE (Siskiyou National Forest)
12 units, trailers to 18', boat launch, lake - no motors, boating, swimming, fishing, hiking, elev. 5400'.
Southeast of Cave Junction. State Highway 199 south 7.0 miles to O'Brien, CR 5560 east 4.0 miles, CR 5828 for 2.0 miles, FSR 48 for 6.0 miles, FSR 4812 for 3.0 miles, FSR 4812.040 for 1.0 mile to campground.

CHEMULT (D-11)

CORRAL SPRINGS (Winema National Forest)
5 units, trailers to 22', primitive, hiking into Sky Lakes or Pelican Butte, mosquitoes, elev. 4900'.

Northwest of Chemult. US Highway 97 north 2.7 miles, FSR 9774 west 1.9 miles.

JACKSON CREEK (Winema National Forest)
12 units, trailers to 22', horse corral, hike into Yamsay Crater, fishing, elev. 4600'.
Southeast of Chemult. US Highway 97 south 24.5 miles, CR 676 northeast 22.1 miles, FSR 49 southeast 5.3 miles.

CHILOQUIN (D-11)

HEAD OF THE RIVER (Winema National Forest)
6 units, trailers to 32', no tables, primitive, fishing, elev. 4600'.
Northeast of Chiloquin. CR 858 northeast 5.0 miles, CR 600 northeast 20.0 miles, FSR 4648 north 1.0 mile.

CHRISTMAS VALLEY (D-11)

GREEN MOUNTAIN (BLM)
4 units, open year round, elev. 5000'.
North of Christmas Valley. Sink Road north to Green Mountain and campground.

COOS BAY (A-11)

NESIKA PARK (Coos County)
20 campsites, pit toilets, picnic facilities, fishing, swimming, hiking.
East of Coos Bay. Coos River Highway 21.0 miles along north shore of Millicoma River. Located 5 miles east of Allegheny.

ROOKE-HIGGINS PARK (Coos County)
18 primitive units, boat ramp, pit toilets, boating, fishing, hiking.
East of Coos Bay. Coos River Highway 10.0 miles along north shore of Millicoma River.

COQUILLE (A-11)

HAM BUNCH CHERRY CREEK (Coos County)
15 campsites, drinking water, community kitchen, stream, fishing, hiking.
Southeast of Coquille. State Highway 42 southeast 9.0 miles, Dora Road east 7.0 miles.

PARK CREEK (BLM)
6 units, water, elev. 500'.
Southeast of Coquille. State Highway 42 south 5.0 miles, east to McKinley, Middle Creek Road north 10.0 miles to campground.

COVE (F-8)

MOSS SPRINGS (Wallowa-Whitman National Forest)
7 units, trailers to 22', picnic area, hiking trails, horse ramp & stall, elev. 5400'.
East of Cove. CR 602 southeast 1.5 miles, FSR 6220 east 6.5 miles.

CRESCENT (D-10)

LAVA FLOW (Deschutes National Forest)
12 units, trailers to 22', on east shore of Davis Lake - speed limits, boating, good fishing, elev. 4400'.
Northwest of Crescent. CR 46 for .5 mile to FSR 62, west .2 mile, FSR 850 north 2.0 miles.

CRESCENT LAKE (C-10)

CONTORTA POINT (Deschutes National Forest)
9 units, trailers to 22', on south end of Crescent Lake, boating, fishing, swimming, water skiing, windsurfing, elev. 4800'.
Northwest of Crescent Lake. CR 61 west 9.0 miles, FSR 46 north 7.0 miles, FSR 62 west .2 mile, FSR 850 north 2.0 miles.

SUMMIT LAKE (Deschutes National Forest)
3 units, trailers to 22', lake, boating, swimming, fishing, hike to Pacific Crest Trail, elev. 5600'.
West of Crescent Lake. CR 61 west 11.5 miles, State Highway 58 northwest 3.0 miles, FSR 60 southwest 5.0 miles, FSR 6010 west 6.0 miles along unimproved road.

CULP CREEK (B-10)

CEDAR CREEK (Umpqua National Forest)
8 units, trailers to 18', picnic facilities, stream, fishing, swimming, nearby hiking, elev. 1600'.
Southeast of Culp Creek. Row River Road #2400 southeast 4.3 miles, CR 2470 southeast 4.0 miles along Brice Creek.

HOBO CAMP (Umpqua National Forest)
2 tent units, stream, swimming, fishing, hiking, elev. 1800'.
Southeast of Culp Creek. Row River Road #2400 southeast 4.3 miles, CR 2470 southeast 7.5 miles along Brice Creek.

LUNDPARK (Umpqua National Forest)
5 units, trailers to 18', picnic facilities, stream, swimming, fishing, hiking, elev. 1700'.
Southeast of Culp Creek. Row River Road #2400 southeast 4.3 miles, CR 2470 southeast 6.9 miles along Brice Creek.

MINERAL (Umpqua National Forest)
2 tent units, picnic facilities, stream, fishing, hiking, elev. 1800'.
Southeast of Culp Creek. Row River Road #2400 southeast .8 mile, CR 2460 south 12.3 miles.

RUJADA (Umpqua National Forest)
8 units, 2 group sites, trailers to 22', picnic area, piped water, stream, flush toilets, play field, swimming, fishing, hiking, horseshoe pits, game field, elev. 1200'.
East of Culp Creek. Row River Road #2400 southeast 4.3 miles, FSR 17 northeast 1.9 miles.

SHARPS CREEK (BLM)
10 units, drinking water, creek, swimming, elev. 1200'.

South of Culp Creek. Dorena/Culp Creek Road 12.0 miles to Culp Creek, Sharps Creek Road south 4.0 miles to campground.

CULVER (D-9)

MONTY (Deschutes National Forest)
39 units, 6 group sites, trailers to 22', piped water, flush toilets, Metolius River, fishing, elev. 2100'.
Northwest of Culver. Culver Highway northeast 9.6 miles, turn at sign for Cove Palisades State Park, FSR 63 to FSR 64, 16 miles to campground.

DALE (E-8)

GOLD DREDGE (Umatilla National Forest)
5 tent units, no drinking water, picnic facilities, on North Fork John Day Wild & Scenic River, fishing, hiking, trail bikes, elev. 4300'.
Northeast of Dale. US Highway 395 northeast 1.0 miles, FSR 55 northwest 5.0 miles, FSR 5506 southeast 1.9 miles.

OLIVE LAKE (Umatilla National Forest)
3 units, trailers to 32', picnic area, lake - speed limits, elev. 6000'.
Southeast of Dale. US Highway 395 northeast 1.0 mile, FSR 55 southeast .6 mile, FSR 10 southeast 26.3 miles, FSR 420 southwest .3 mile.

ORIENTAL CREEK (Umatilla National Forest)
5 tent units, on North Fork John Day Wild & Scenic River, fishing, hiking, no water, elev. 3500'.
Northeast of Dale. US Highway 395 northeast 1.0 miles, FSR 55 northwest 5.0 miles, FSR 5506 southeast 8.0 miles.

TOLLBRIDGE (Umatilla National Forest)
7 units, trailers to 32', piped water, stream, fishing, at mouth of Desolation Creek, elev. 3800'.
East of Dale. US Highway 395 northeast 1.0 mile, FSR 55 southeast .6 mile, FSR 10 southeast .1 mile.

WELCH CREEK (Umatilla National Forest)
1 unit, trailer to 22', picnic area, fishing, elev. 4500'.
Southeast of Dale. US Highway 395 northeast 1.0 mile, FSR 55 southeast .6 mile, FSR 10 southeast 13.9 miles.

DETROIT (C-9)

ELK LAKE (Willamette National Forest)
12 units, no trailers, stream, primitive boat launch, rough road, fishing, swimming, hiking, elev. 4000'.
North of Detroit. FSR 46 northeast 4.6 miles, FSR 4696 north 7.1 miles, FSR 2209 northwest 9.5 miles, FSR 360 southwest .4 mile.

PIETY ISLAND (Willamette National Forest)
12 tent units, boat-in only, on Detroit Reservoir, swimming, fishing, water skiing, primitive, elev. 1600'.
Southwest of Detroit. By boat 1.1 miles southwest on lake.

UPPER ARM (Willamette National Forest)
5 units, lake, boating, swimming, fishing, elev. 1600'.
Northeast of Detroit. FSR 46 northeast 1.1 mile. On Breitenbush Arm of Detroit Lake.

DIAMOND LAKE (C-11)

INLET (Umpqua National Forest)
Campsites, lake, fishing, hiking, water skiing.
North of Diamond Lake. Road #268 north, campground is located near Lemolo Lake.

DUFUR (D-8)

EIGHTMILE CROSSING (Mt. Hood National Forest)
14 units, trailers to 18', picnic area, stream, fishing, elev. 4200'.
Southwest of Dufur. CR 1 southwest 12.0 miles, FSR 44 west 4.3 miles, FSR 4430 north .6 mile.

FIFTEEN MILE (Mt. Hood National Forest)
4 units, trailers to 18', stream, elev. 4600'.

Southwest of Dufur. CR 1 southwest 12.0 miles, FSR 44 west 6.0 miles, FSR 2730 south 3.5 miles.

KNEBAL SPRINGS (Mt. Hood National Forest)
6 units, trailers to 22', elev. 4000'.
West of Dufur. CR 1 southwest 12.0 miles, FSR 44 west 4.3 miles, FSR 4430 north 4.0 miles, FSR 1720 southwest 1.0 mile.

LOWER CROSSING (Mt. Hood National Forest)
2 units, trailers to 18', picnic area, stream, fishing, elev. 3800'
Southwest of Dufur. CR 1 southwest 12.0 miles, FSR 44 west 4.0 miles, FSR 4440 north 1.0 mile.

PEBBLE FORD (Mt. Hood National Forest)
5 units, trailers to 18', stream, elev. 4000'.
Southwest of Dufur. CR 1 southwest 12.0 miles, FSR 44 west 5.0 miles, FSR 131 south .5 mile.

ELGIN (E-8)

WOODLAND (Umatilla National Forest)
7 units, trailers to 22', picnic facilities, no water, elev. 5200'.
Northwest of Elgin. State Highway 204 northwest 16.0 miles.

ENTERPRISE (F-8)

BUCKHORN (Wallowa-Whitman National Forest)
6 units, trailers to 22', picnic area, piped water, spring, stock ramp, elev. 5200'.
Northeast of Enterprise. State Highway 82 south 3.0 miles, CR 772 northeast 5.2 miles, CR 798 northeast 25.8 miles, FSR 46 northeast 9.6 miles to campground.

COYOTE (Wallowa-Whitman National Forest)
21 units, trailers to 22', primitive, elev. 4800'.
Northeast of Enterprise. State Highway 3 north 15.0 miles, FSR 46 northeast 30.0 miles.

DOUGHERTY (Wallowa-Whitman National Forest)
10 units, trailers to 22', stream, elev. 4900'.
Northeast of Enterprise. State Highway 3 north 15.0 miles, FSR 46 northeast 37.0 miles,

MUD CREEK (BLM)
Campsites, restrooms, boat ramp, Grande Ronde River.
Northwest of Enterprise. State Highway 3 north 30.0 miles to Flora, Lost Prairie Road west 3.0 miles, Troy Road northwest 3.0 miles then southwest 4.0 miles to campground.

VIGNE (Wallowa-Whitman National Forest)
12 units, trailers to 22', well, stream, fishing, primitive, elev. 3000'.
Northeast of Enterprise. State Highway 3 north 15.0 miles, FSR 46 northeast 22.0 miles.

ESTACADA (B-8)

ALDER FLAT (Mt. Hood National Forest)
6 tent units, picnic area, hike-in only, on Clackamas River, fishing, hiking trails, elev. 1300'.
Southeast of Estacada. State Highway 224 southeast 25.8 miles, Trail #574 west .7 mile.

BREITENBUSH LAKE (Mt. Hood National Forest)
25 units, trailers to 18', lake - no motors, boating, swimming, fishing, trails, elev. 5200'.
Southeast of Estacada. State Highway 224 southeast 26.7 miles, FSR 46 south 28.6 miles, FSR 4220 south 8.4 miles, access road is primitive and not maintained.

CAMP TEN (Mt. Hood National Forest)
6 units, trailers to 18', lake - no motors, boating, fishing, trails, elev. 5000'.
Southeast of Estacada. State Highway 224 southeast 26.7 miles, FSR 46 south 28.6 miles, FSR 4220 south 6.1 miles.

EAST TWIN LAKE (Mt. Hood National Forest)
3 units, hike-in, fishing, swimming, elev. 4100'.

Southeast of Estacada. State Highway 224 southeast 26.7 miles, FSR 46 south 3.7 miles, FSR 63 south 5.4 miles, FSR 708/6340 southwest 8.0 miles, FSR S739/6431 southwest 3.5 miles, Trails #551, #558 and #573 for 10.0 miles to campground.

FRAZIER TURN AROUND (Mt. Hood National Forest)
8 tent units, trailhead to Rock Lakes, elev. 4700'.
Southeast of Estacada. State Highway 224 southeast 27.0 miles, FSR 57 east 7.5 miles, FSR 58 northeast 7.6 miles, FSR S457/4610 northeast 2.2 miles, FSR S456/4610240 west 4.2 miles. Primitive road.

HAMBONE SPRINGS (Mt. Hood National Forest)
7 tent units, creek, elev. 4200'.
Southeast of Estacada. State Highway 224 southeast 7.0 miles, FSR S403/4611 southeast 7.9 miles, FSR S469/4610 southeast 17.2 miles.

HIGH ROCK SPRING (Mt. Hood National Forest)
7 tent units, elev. 4400'.
Southeast of Estacada. State Highway 224 southeast 27.0 miles, FSR 57 east 7.5 miles, FSR 58 northeast 10.5 miles.

HORSESHOE LAKE (Mt. Hood National Forest)
4 tent units, lake - no motors, boating, swimming, fishing, elev. 5200'.
Southeast of Estacada. State Highway 224 southeast 26.7 miles, FSR 46 south 28.6 miles, FSR 4220 south 8.3 miles.

LAKE LENORE (Mt. Hood National Forest)
2 tent units, hike-in only, fishing, lake, trails, elev. 4800'.
Southeast of Estacada. State Highway 224 southeast 26.7 miles, FSR 46 south 3.7 miles, FSR 63 south 5.4 miles, FSR 708/6340 southwest 2.9 miles, FSR 708A for 2.0 miles, Trails #553 and #555 for 6.0 miles. Steep trail to lake.

LITTLE FAN CREEK (Mt. Hood National Forest)
3 units, some trailers, stream, fishing, hiking, elev. 1600'.
Southeast of Estacada. State Highway 224 southeast 26.7

miles, FSR 46 south 3.7 miles, FSR 63 for 4.6 miles. Located at mouth of Hot Springs Fork of Collawash River.

LOOKOUT SPRINGS (Mt. Hood National Forest)
6 units, trailers to 18', trails, elev. 4000'.
Southeast of Estacada. State Highway 224 southeast 7.6 miles, FSR S403/4611 southeast 7.9 miles, FSR S469/4610 northeast 5.1 miles.

LOWER LAKE (Mt. Hood National Forest)
9 units, trailers to 18', trails, elev. 4600'.
Southeast of Estacada. State Highway 224 southeast 26.7 miles, FSR 46 south 28.6 miles, FSR 4220 south 4.5 miles.

NORTH FORK CROSSING (Mt. Hood National Forest)
11 units, trailers to 18', stream, fishing, elev. 2000'.
Southeast of Estacada. State Highway 224 southeast 7.0 miles, FSR S403/4611 southeast 8.0 miles, FSR S457 northwest .5 mile. Located on North Fork of Clackamas River.

OLALLIE MEADOW (Mt. Hood National Forest)
7 units, trailers to 18', no water, trails, elev. 4500'.
Southeast of Estacada. State Highway 224 southeast 26.7 miles, FSR 46 south 28.6 miles, FSR 4220 south 1.4 miles.

PANSY LAKE (Mt. Hood National Forest)
3 tent units, hike-in only, lake, elev. 4000'.
Southeast of Estacada. State Highway 224 southeast 26.7 miles, FSR 46 south 3.7 miles, FSR 63 south 5.4 miles, FSR 708/6340 southwest 8.0 miles, Trail #551 for 1.0 mile.

PEGLEG FALLS (Mt. Hood National Forest)
10 units, trailers to 18', no water, on Hot Springs Fork of Collawash River, fish ladder, near Bagby Hot Springs Trailhead, fishing, elev. 2000'.
Southeast of Estacada. State Highway 224 southeast 26.7 miles, FSR 46 south 3.7 miles, FSR 63 south 3.4 miles, FSR 70 southwest 6.0 miles.

RAAB (Mt. Hood National Forest)
25 units, trailers to 22', river, fishing, elev. 1500'.
Southeast of Estacada. State Highway 224 southeast 26.7 miles, FSR 46 southeast 3.7 miles, FSR 63 southeast 1.0 mile.

RIVERFORD (Mt. Hood National Forest)
10 units, trailers to 18', river, swimming, fishing, trails, elev. 1500'.
Southeast of Estacada. State Highway 224 southeast 26.7 miles, FSR 46 south 3.5 miles.

ROUND LAKE (Mt. Hood National Forest)
6 tent units, hike-in only, lake - no motors, swimming, fishing, elev. 3200'.
Southeast of Estacada. State Highway 224 southeast 26.7 miles, FSR 46 south 3.7 miles, FSR 63 southeast 12.4 miles, FSR 6370 southeast 6.7 miles, hike-in .3 mile.

SHELLROCK CREEK (Mt. Hood National Forest)
10 units, fishing, elev. 2300'.
Southeast of Estacada. State Highway 224 southeast 27.0 miles, FSR 57 east 7.5 miles, FSR 58 north .4 mile.

SHINING LAKE (Mt. Hood National Forest)
11 tent units, hike-in only, fishing, trails, elev. 4200'.
Southeast of Estacada. State Highway 224 southeast 27.0 miles, FSR 57 east 7.5 miles, FSR 58 northeast 7.6 miles, FSR S457/4610 northeast 2.2 miles, FSR S456/4610240 west 7.1 miles, Indian Ridge Trail for 4.0 miles.

SILVER KING LAKE (Mt. Hood National Forest)
1 tent unit, hike-in only, fishing, elev. 4100'.
Southeast of Estacada. State Highway 224 southeast 26.7 miles, FSR 46 south 3.7 miles, FSR 63 south 3.4 miles, FSR 70 southwest 6.3 miles, Trails #544 and #520 for 7.5 miles to campground. Also accessible via Trail #546.

TWIN SPRINGS (Mt. Hood National Forest)
6 tent units, trails, cold water spring, elev. 4200'.
Southeast of Estacada. State Highway 224 southeast 7.0 miles, FSR S403/4611 southeast 7.9 miles, FSR S469/4610 southeast 10.9 miles.

WELCOME LAKE (Mt. Hood National Forest)
2 tent units, hike-in only, lake, fishing, hiking, elev. 4200'.
Southeast of Estacada. State Highway 224 southeast 26.7 miles, FSR 46 south 3.7 miles, FSR 63 south 14.5 miles, Trail #554 for 4.0 miles to lake.

WEST TWIN LAKE (Mt. Hood National Forest)
2 tent units, hike-in, lake, swimming, fishing, trails, elev. 4200'.
Southeast of Estacada. State Highway 224 southeast 26.7 miles, FSR 46 south 3.7 miles, FSR 63 south 5.4 miles, FSR 708/6340 southwest 8.0 miles, FSR S739/6341 southwest 3.5 miles, Trails #551, #558 and #573 for 10.0 miles to campground.

FLORENCE (A-10)

NORTH FORK SIUSLAW (Siuslaw National Forest)
5 tent units, river, fishing, primitive, elev. 100'.
Northeast of Florence. State Highway 36 east 1.0 mile, CR 5070 northeast 13.5 miles, FSR 715 east .1 mile.

FORT ROCK (D-11)

CABIN LAKE (Deschutes National Forest)
14 units, trailers to 22', piped water, bird watching, elev. 4500'.
North of Fort Rock. FSR 18 north 9.8 miles.

CHINA HAT (Deschutes National Forest)
14 units, trailers to 32', piped water, elev. 5100'.
North of Fort Rock. FSR 18 north 20.8 miles.

FOX (E-9)

BEECH CREEK (Malheur National Forest)
5 units, trailers to 18', fishing, primitive, elev. 4500'.
Southeast of Fox. US Highway 395 south 6.0 miles.

GARDINER (A-10)

SMITH RIVER FALLS (BLM)
8 units, berry picking, fishing, elev. 100'.
Northeast of Gardiner. US Highway 101 north 1.5 miles, Smith River Road east 27.0 miles.

TWIN SISTERS PARK (International Paper)
10 campsites, trailers okay, fishing, at John H. Hinman Tree Farm.
East of Gardiner. US Highway 101 north 1.5 miles, Smith River Road east 44.0 miles.

GLIDE (B-11)

BIG TWIN LAKES (Umpqua National Forest)
Campsites, fishing, hiking trail.
East of Glide. Follow State Highway 138 east to FSR 4770 and Big Twin Lakes. Campground is 40.0 miles east of Glide.

BOULDER FLAT (Umpqua National Forest)
11 units, some trailers, picnic area, stream, fishing, hiking, elev. 1600'.
East of Glide. State Highway 138 east 34.0 miles.

COOLWATER CAMP (Umpqua National Forest)
7 units, trailers to 24', picnic facilities, well, river, fishing, nearby hiking trails, swimming, elev. 1300'.
Southeast of Glide. Little River Road #17 southeast 15.5 miles.

EMILE SHELTER (Umpqua National Forest)
1 unit w/shelter, trailers to 22', stream, fishing, elev. 4000'.
Southeast of Glide. Little River Road #17 southeast 16.5 miles, FSR 2703 north 8.9 miles.

HEMLOCK LAKE (Umpqua National Forest)
13 units, trailers to 35', picnic facilities, no drinking water, lake - no motors, nearby boat ramp, swimming, fishing, loop trail, elev. 4400'.

Southeast of Glide. Little River Road #17 southeast 32.0 miles.

WHITE CREEK (Umpqua National Forest)
4 walk-in campsites, well, river, swimming, fishing, trails, elev. 1600'.
Southeast of Glide. Little River Road #17 southeast 16.8 miles, FSR 2792 east .5 mile.

GOLD BEACH (A-12)

LOBSTER CREEK (Siskiyou National Forest)
5 units, picnic area, boat ramp.
East of Gold Beach. FSR 33 east 8.5 miles.

GOVERNMENT CAMP (C-8)

BARLOW CREEK (Mt. Hood National Forest)
5 units, trailers to 18', fishing, elev. 3100'.
East of Government Camp. US Highway 26 east 2.0 miles, State Highway 35 north 4.5 miles, FSR 3530 southeast 4.2 miles.

BARLOW CROSSING (Mt. Hood National Forest)
5 units, trailers to 18', stream, fishing, elev. 3100'.
East of Government Camp. US Highway 26 east 2.0 miles, State Highway 35 north 4.5 miles, FSR 3530 southeast 5.2 miles.

BEAR PAW (Mt. Hood National Forest)
2 tent units, stream, elev. 3200'.
Southeast of Government Camp. US Highway 26 southeast 14.0 miles.

DEVILS HALF ACRE (Mt. Hood National Forest)
4 units, trailers to 18', stream, fishing, elev. 3600'.
Northeast of Government Camp. US Highway 26 east 2.0 miles, State Highway 35 north 4.5 miles, FSR 3530 east 1.0 mile.

FIR TREE (Mt. Hood National Forest)
5 tent units, not maintained, creek, trailhead to Vida Lake, elev. 4500'.
South of Government Camp. US Highway 26 east 1.0 mile, FSR 32/2613 southwest 5.1 miles.

GRINDSTONE (Mt. Hood National Forest)
3 units, trailers to 18', stream, elev. 3400'.
East of Government Camp. US Highway 26 east 2.0 miles, State Highway 35 north 4.5 miles, FSR 3530 east 3.0 miles.

KINZEL LAKE (Mt. Hood National Forest)
5 tent units, not maintained, creek, swimming, trails, elev. 4400'.
Southwest of Government Camp. US Highway 26 east 1.0 mile. FSR 32/2613 southwest 10.6 miles. Primitive road.

LINNEY CREEK (Mt. Hood National Forest)
4 tent units, creek, fishing, trails, elev. 2800'.
Southwest of Government Camp. US Highway 26 southeast 15.0 miles, FSR 42 south 4.0 miles, FSR S457/4610 southwest 11.7 miles, FSR 407 north 4.3 miles.

MEDITATION POINT (Mt. Hood National Forest)
3 tent units, boat-in or hike-in only, lake - speed limits, boating, swimming, fishing, elev. 3200'.
South of Government Camp. US Highway 26 southeast 15.0 miles, FSR 42 south 8.0 miles, FSR 57 west 6.0 miles, boat or hike 1.0 mile north.

SUMMIT LAKE (Mt. Hood National Forest)
6 tent units, lake - no motors, swimming, elev. 4000'.
Southeast of Government Camp. US Highway 26 southeast 15.0 miles, FSR 42 south 13.0 miles, FSR 141 southeast 1.0 mile.

WHITE RIVER STATION (Mt. Hood National Forest)
5 units, trailers to 18', stream, fishing, elev. 2800'.
Southeast of Government Camp. US Highway 26 east 2.0 miles, State Highway 35 north 4.5 miles, FSR 3530 east 7.2 miles.

HAINES (E-9)

N. FORK ANTHONY CREEK (Wallowa-Whitman National Forest)
4 tent sites, fishing, hiking, primitive, elev. 5300'.
Northeast of Haines. State Highway 30 north 4.0 miles, FSR 73 east 11.0 miles.

HALFWAY (F-9)

DUCK LAKE (Wallowa-Whitman National Forest)
2 units, lake, boating, swimming, fishing, hiking, rough roads, elev. 5700'.
Northeast of Halfway. State Highway 86 east 9.2 miles, FSR 39 north 13.0 miles, FSR 66 west 5.8 miles, FSR 3980 north .7 mile.

FISH LAKE (Wallowa-Whitman National Forest)
23 units, trailers to 22', piped water, stream, boating, swimming, fishing, elev. 6600'.
North of Halfway. CR 733 north 5.0 miles, FSR 66 north 18.6 miles.

McBRIDE (Wallowa-Whitman National Forest)
5 units, trailers to 18', creek. elev. 4800'.
Northwest of Halfway. State Highway 413 northwest 5.0 miles, FSR 7710 west 2.5 miles, FSR 77 west 2.1 miles.

TWIN LAKES (Wallowa-Whitman National Forest)
9 units, trailers to 22', lake, boating, swimming, fishing, hiking, elev. 6500'.
Northeast of Halfway. State Highway 86 east 9.2 miles, FSR 39 north 13.0 miles, FSR 66 west 10.9 miles.

HEBO (A-8)

CASTLE ROCK (Siuslaw National Forest)
4 units, well, stream, fishing, primitive, elev. 200'.
Southeast of Hebo. State Highway 22 southeast 4.7 miles.

MT. HEBO (Siuslaw National Forest)
4 tent sites on top of Mt. Hebo, elev. 3000'.

East of Hebo. State Highway 22 southeast .3 mile, FSR 14 east 9.6 miles, FSR 14115 east .1 mile.

HEPPNER (D-8)

FAIRVIEW (Umatilla National Forest)
5 tent sites, some trailers, picnic area, drinking water, elev. 4300'.
South of Heppner. State Highway 207 south 34.0 miles.

PENLAND LAKE (Umatilla National Forest)
5 side-by-side sites, picnic area, swimming, no water, boat launch, lake - electric motors only, minimal facilities, fishing, elev. 4950'.
Southeast of Heppner. CR 678 southeast 19.0 miles, FSR 53 south 2.5 miles, FSR 21 south 2.9 miles, FSR 2103 east 2.8 miles, FSR 2103-030 northeast .3 mile.

HOOD RIVER (C-8)

KINGSLEY RESERVOIR (Hood River County)
20 tent sites, pit toilets, no water, fishing, boat ramp & dock, hiking, mountain biking.
Southwest of Hood River. Follow Kingsley Road southwest out of town to FSR N205 and reservoir.

IDLEYLD PARK (B-11)

WILLIAMS CREEK (Umpqua National Forest)
2 units, picnic facilities, no drinking water, stream, fly fishing, swimming, hiking, elev. 1100'.
Northeast of Idleyld Park. State Highway 138 southeast 8.0 miles, FSR 4710 northeast 3.5 miles, FSR 480 northeast 5.3 miles.

IMNAHA (F-7)

HAT POINT (Wallowa-Whitman National Forest)
4 units, picnic area, hiking, stock ramp, outstanding view, elev. 7000'.
Southeast of Imnaha. FSR 4240 southeast 23.4 miles, FSR 315 east .7 mile.

SADDLE CREEK (Wallowa-Whitman National Forest)
6 units, trailers to 18', view, elev. 6600'.
Southeast of Imnaha. FSR 4240 southeast 19.7 miles to campground.

JACKSONVILLE (B-12)

HARR POINT CAMP (Rogue River National Forest)
5 tent units, boat-in/walk-in only, boating, swimming, fishing, trails, elev. 2100'.
Southwest of Jacksonville. State Highway 238 southwest 8.0 miles, CR 10 southwest 16.0 miles, walk to campsites from here or boat-in.

LATGAWA COVE CAMP (Rogue River National Forest)
5 tent units, boat-in/walk-in only, boating, swimming, fishing, trails, elev. 2100'.
Southwest of Jacksonville. State Highway 238 southwest 8.0 miles, CR 10 southwest 14.0 miles, FSR 1075 east 1.0 mile, walk to campsites from here or boat-in.

TIPSU TYEE CAMP (Rogue River National Forest)
5 tent units, boat-in/walk-in only, lake, boating, swimming, fishing, trails, elev. 2100'.
Southwest of Jacksonville. State Highway 238 southwest 8.0 miles, CR 10 southwest 14.0 miles, walk to campsites from here or boat-in.

WRANGLE (Rogue River National Forest)
5 units, trailers to 18', picnic area w/community kitchen, swimming, hiking, elev. 6400'.
Southeast of Jacksonville. State Highway 238 southwest 8.0 miles, CR 10 south 10.0 miles, FSR 20 east 25.0 miles, FSR 2030 northwest 1.0 mile.

JOHN DAY (E-10)

CANYON MEADOWS (Malheur National Forest)
18 units, trailers to 18', picnic area, piped water, reservoir - no motors, boating, hiking, fishing, wilderness access, elev. 5100'.

Southeast of John Day. US Highway 395 south 10.0 miles, FSR 15 southeast 9.0 miles, FSR 1520 northeast 5.0 miles.

RAY COLE (Malheur National Forest)
1 unit, trailers to 22', no drinking water, stream, fishing, wilderness access, elev. 4300'.
Southeast of John Day. US Highway 395 south 10.0 miles, FSR 15 southeast 3.0 miles, FSR 1510 north 1.0 mile.

WICKIUP (Malheur National Forest)
9 units, trailers to 18', picnic area, piped water, stream, fishing, elev. 4300'.
Southeast of John Day. US Highway 395 south 10.0 miles, FSR 15 southeast 8.0 miles.

JORDAN VALLEY (F-11)

LESLIE GULCH (BLM)
8 units, picnic sites, on Owyhee River, boating, swimming, boat ramp, elev. 2800'.
Northwest of Jordan Valley. US Highway 95 north 18.0 miles, left 11.0 miles, Leslie Gulch Road 7.0 miles west to campground.

JOSEPH (F-8)

EVERGREEN (Wallowa-Whitman National Forest)
17 units, trailers to 32', river, swimming, fishing, hiking, in Hells Canyon National Recreation Area, elev. 4500'.
Southeast of Joseph. State Highway 350 east 7.7 miles, FSR 39 south 28.8 miles, FSR 3960 southwest 8.0 miles.

HURRICANE CREEK (Wallowa-Whitman National Forest)
8 units, trailers to 18', picnic area, stream, fishing, trails into Eagle Cap Wilderness, primitive, elev. 4600'.
Southwest of Joseph. Take County Road southwest 3.5 miles, FSR 8205 south .5 mile.

KIMBERLEY (D-9)

BIG BEND (BLM)
4 units, no drinking water, year round, elev. 1500'.
Northeast of Kimberley. County Road northeast 3.0 miles to campground.

LONE PINE (BLM)
4 units, no drinking water, year round, elev. 1500'.
Northeast of Kimberley. County Road northeast 4.0 miles to campground.

KLAMATH FALLS (C-12)

COLDSPRINGS (Winema National Forest)
2 tent units, primitive, trailhead access to Sky Lakes Wilderness & Pelican Butte, elev. 5800'.
Northwest of Klamath Falls. State Highway 140 northwest 30.0 miles, FSR 3651 north 11.0 miles.

ODESSA (Winema National Forest)
6 units, trailers to 22', stream, boat launch, fishing, primitive, elev. 4100'.
Northwest of Klamath Falls. State Highway 140 northwest 22.0 miles, FSR 3639 northeast .9 mile.

SEVENMILE MARSH (Winema National Forest)
2 tent units, trailhead access to Sky Lakes Wilderness, elev. 5500'.
Northwest of Klamath Falls. State Highway 140 west to CR 531, north 1.5 miles, FSR 3334 for 6.5 miles to campground.

SURVEYOR (BLM)
8 units, drinking water, elev. 5160'.
West of Klamath Falls. US Highway 97 south 3.0 miles, State Highway 66 southwest 13.0 miles, Howard Prairie Lake Road 14.0 miles to campground.

LA GRANDE (E-8)

GRANDVIEW (Wallowa-Whitman National Forest)
4 units, hiking, primitive, elev. 6000'.
North of La Grande. I-84 west 20.0 miles, FSR 31 north 20.0 miles, FSR 3120 south 3.2 miles.

RIVER (Wallowa-Whitman National Forest)
6 units, trailers to 22', well, picnic area, river, fishing, primitive, elev. 3800'.
Southwest of La Grande. I-84 west 9.1 miles, State Highway 244 southwest 12.9 miles, FSR 51 south 8.5 miles, FSR 5125 south 9.0 miles.

SPOOL CART (Wallowa-Whitman National Forest)
5 units, trailers to 22', river, fishing, primitive, elev. 3700'.
Southwest of La Grande. I-84 west 9.1 miles, State Highway 244 southwest 12.9 miles, FSR 51 south 4.5 miles.

TIME AND A HALF (Wallowa-Whitman National Forest)
5 units, trailers to 22', river, fishing, primitive, elev. 3800'.
Southwest of La Grande. I-84 west 9.1 miles, State Highway 244 southwest 12.9 miles, FSR 51 south 6.5 miles.

WOODLEY (Wallowa-Whitman National Forest)
7 units, trailers to 22', picnic area, piped water, river, fishing, hiking trails, primitive, elev. 4500'.
Southwest of La Grande. I-84 west 9.1 miles, State Highway 244 southwest 12.9 miles, FSR 51 south 16.0 miles, FSR 5125 southeast 5.0 miles.

LAKEVIEW (D-12)

CINDER HILL (Fremont National Forest)
5 units, boat launch, boating, fishing, elev. 5100'.
Southwest of Lakeview. State Highway 140 west 7.0 miles, CR 1-13 south 4.0 miles, CR 1-11 west 32.0 miles, FSR 4017 west 10.0 miles.

COTTONWOOD MEADOWS (Fremont National Forest)
26 units, trailers to 22', piped water, lake - electric motors

only, boating, hiking, swimming, fishing, elev. 6200'.
Northwest of Lakeview. State Highway 140 west 20.0 miles, FSR 3870 northeast 5.0 miles.

DEEP CREEK (Fremont National Forest)
6 units, trailers okay, stream, fishing, elev. 5600'.
Southeast of Lakeview. US Highway 395 north 5.4 miles, State Highway 140 east 6.5 miles, FSR 3915 south 16.0 miles, Road 4015 to campground.

MUD CREEK (Fremont National Forest)
7 units, trailers to 18', piped water, stream, good fishing, remote, elev. 6600'.
Northeast of Lakeview. US Highway 395 north 5.4 miles, State Highway 140 east 9.0 miles, FSR 3615 north 6.1 miles.

WILLOW CREEK (Fremont National Forest)
8 units, trailers to 22', well, stream, good fishing, remote, elev. 5800'.
Southeast of Lakeview. US Highway 395 north 5.4 miles, State Highway 140 east 6.5 miles, FSR 3915 south 10.1 miles, Road 4011 to campground.

LaPINE (D-10)

BULL BEND (Deschutes National Forest)
6 tent units, on Deschutes River, fishing, elev. 4400'.
Northwest of LaPine. US Highway 97 northeast 2.4 miles, CR 43 west 8.0 miles, FSR 4370 southwest 1.5 miles.

COW MEADOW (Deschutes National Forest)
20 units, trailers to 22', on Deschutes River, at north end of Crane Prairie Reservoir - speed limits, boating, fishing, elev. 4400'.
Northwest of LaPine. US Highway 97 northeast 2.4 miles, CR 43 west 11.0 miles, FSR 42 northeast 3.0 miles.

CRANE PRAIRIE (Deschutes National Forest)
147 units, trailers to 22', well, on Crane Prairie Reservoir - speed limits, boating, fishing, elev. 4400'.
Northwest of LaPine. US Highway 97 northeast 2.4 miles,

CR 43 west 11.0 miles, FSR 42 west 6.0 miles, FSR 4270 north 4.5 miles.

CULTUS CORRAL (Deschutes National Forest)
25 units, trailers okay, reservations advised (503) 388-5664, river, no tables, horse corral, boat launch, boating, swimming, fishing, water skiing, hiking, elev. 4400'.
Southwest of LaPine. US Highway 97 northeast 2.4 miles, CR 43 west 11.0 miles, FSR 42 west 9.5 miles, CR 46 north 8.0 miles, FSR 620 west .5 mile.

FALL RIVER (Deschutes National Forest)
10 units, trailers to 22', stream, fly fishing only, elev. 4000'.
Northwest of LaPine. US Highway 97 northeast 2.4 miles, CR 43 west 11.0 miles, FSR 42 northeast .3 mile.

JONES WELL (Deschutes National Forest)
3 units, very primitive, no facilities, elev. 5100'.
East of LaPine. FSR 22 east 11.0 miles, FSR 2222 south .5 mile.

NORTH COVE (Deschutes National Forest)
6 tent units, hike-in/boat-in only, on Paulina Lake - speed limits, boating, fishing, trails, elev. 6300'.
East of LaPine. US Highway 97 north 5.0 miles, CR 21 east 13.1 miles, boat north 1.4 miles or follow Trail #57 to northwest shore of lake and campground.

PRINGLE FALLS (Deschutes National Forest)
7 units, trailers to 22', on Deschutes River, fishing, elev. 4300'.
Northwest of LaPine. US Highway 97 northeast 2.4 miles, CR 43 west 7.2 miles, FSR 30500 northeast .7 mile.

RESERVOIR (Deschutes National Forest)
28 units, trailers to 22', on south shore of Wickiup Reservoir, boating, fishing, elev. 4400'.
West of LaPine. US Highway 97 northeast 2.4 miles, CR 43 west 10.0 miles, FSR 42 west 8.0 miles, FSR 46 south 5.0 miles, FSR 44 east 1.7 miles.

SHEEP BRIDGE (Deschutes National Forest)
12 units, trailers to 22', well, on Deschutes River, at Wickiup Reservoir, fishing, elev. 4400'.
West of LaPine. US Highway 97 northeast 2.4 miles, CR 43 west 10.0 miles, FSR 42 west 5.3 miles, FSR 4260 west .6 mile.

WICKIUP BUTTE (Deschutes National Forest)
7 units, trailers to 22', on east shore of Wickiup Reservoir, boating, fishing, elev. 4400'.
West of LaPine. US Highway 97 northeast 2.4 miles, CR 43 west 10.0 miles, FSR 42 southwest 5.3 miles, FSR 4260 west 1.0 mile.

WYETH (Deschutes National Forest)
3 units, trailers to 22', no tables, river, fishing, elev. 4300'.
Northwest of LaPine. US Highway 97 northeast 2.4 miles, CR 43 west 7.0 miles, FSR 4370 south .1 mile.

LOSTINE (F-8)

FRENCH CAMP (Wallowa-Whitman National Forest)
4 tent sites, stream, fishing, hiking, primitive, elev. 5300'.
South of Lostine. CR 551 south 7.0 miles, FSR 8210 south 7.0 miles.

LILLYVILLE (Wallowa-Whitman National Forest)
2 units, trailers okay, stream, trailheads to wilderness, elev. 5300'.
South of Lostine. CR 551 south 7.0 miles, FSR 8210 south 8.0 miles.

SHADY (Wallowa-Whitman National Forest)
16 units, trailers to 18', river, swimming, fishing, trailheads to wilderness, primitive, elev. 5400'.
South of Lostine. CR 551 south 7.0 miles, FSR 8210 south 10.0 miles.

TWO PAN (Wallowa-Whitman National Forest)
9 units, trailers to 18', river, swimming, fishing, trailheads to wilderness, primitive, elev. 5600'.
South of Lostine. CR 551 south 7.0 miles, FSR 8210 south 10.8 miles.

WILLIAMSON (Wallowa-Whitman National Forest)
10 units, trailers to 18', river, swimming, fishing, trailheads to wilderness, elev. 5000'.
South of Lostine. CR 551 south 7.0 miles, FSR 8210 south 4.0 miles.

LOWELL (B-10)

DOLLY VARDEN (Willamette National Forest)
5 tent units, stream, fishing, swimming, hiking, elev. 1000'.
Northeast of Lowell. CR 6220 north 1.8 miles, CR 6240 east 9.9 miles, FSR 181 east .5 mile.

UPPER END FALL CREEK LAKE (Corps)
40 units, pit toilets, picnic facilities, boat ramp, on east end of Fall Creek Lake.
Northeast of Lowell. CR 6220 north 1.8 miles, Big Fall Creek Road northeast 7.0 miles to east end of lake and campground.

MARIAL (B-11)

TUCKER FLAT (BLM)
10 units, boating, swimming, fishing, elev. 650'.
At Marial. Located at Marial, on the Rogue River.

MAUPIN (D-8)

CLEAR CREEK (Mt. Hood National Forest)
6 units, trailers to 18', creek, fishing, elev. 3000'.
Northwest of Maupin. State Highway 216 west 28.0 miles, FSR 2130 north 3.0 miles, FSR 260 east .5 mile.

KEEPS MILL (Mt. Hood National Forest)
4 tent units, stream, fishing, elev. 2600'.
Northwest of Maupin. State Highway 216 west 24.0 miles, FSR 2120 north 3.0 miles.

McCUBBINS GULCH (Mt. Hood National Forest)
5 units, trailers to 18', stream, fishing, primitive, elev. 3000'.

Northwest of Maupin. State Highway 216 west 24.5 miles, FSR 2110 east 1.0 mile, FSR 230 northeast .5 mile.

McKENZIE BRIDGE (C-10)

ALDER SPRINGS (Willamette National Forest)
7 units, no trailers, stream, trail to Linton Lake, elev. 3600'.
East of McKenzie Bridge. State Highway 126 east 4.3 miles, State Highway 242 east 8.2 miles.

FISH LAKE (Willamette National Forest)
8 units, trailers to 22', piped water, lake - no motors, swimming, fishing, near lava beds, elev. 3200'.
Northeast of McKenzie Bridge. State Highway 126 northeast 22.4 miles, FSR 1374 west .1 mile. Lake recedes in summer.

LAKES END (Willamette National Forest)
17 tent units, boat-in only, on Smith Reservoir - speed limits, boating, fishing, swimming, elev. 3000'.
Northwest of McKenzie Bridge. State Highway 126 northwest 13.2 miles, FSR 1477 northwest 3.3 miles, boat north 1.8 miles on Smith Reservoir.

LIMBERLOST (Willamette National Forest)
14 units, trailers okay, picnic area, creek, fishing, elev. 1800'.
East of McKenzie Bridge. State Highway 126 east 4.3 miles, State Highway 242 east .5 mile.

MEDICAL SPRINGS (F-8)

TAMARACK (Wallowa-Whitman National Forest)
10 units, trailers to 22', piped water, stream, fishing, elev. 4600'.
East of Medical Springs. FSR 6700 southeast 15.7 miles, FSR 7700 east .3 mile.

TWO COLOR (Wallowa-Whitman National Forest)
14 units, trailers to 22', piped water, stream, fishing, elev. 4800'.

East of Medical Springs. FSR 6700 southeast 15.5 miles, FSR 7755 northeast 1.5 miles.

MEHAMA (C-9)

SHADY COVE (Willamette National Forest)
11 units, no trailers, on Little North Santiam River, fishing, elev. 1400'.
East of Mehama. State Highway 22 east .9 mile, CR 967 east 15.3 miles, FSR S80 east 1.1 miles, FSR 581 east 2.1 miles.

MINAM (F-7)

MINAM (BLM)
4 units, drinking water, boat ramp, year round, elev. 2600'.
East of Minam. State Highway 82 east .2 mile. Adjacent to Wallowa River.

MITCHELL (D-9)

ALLEN CREEK (Ochoco National Forest)
5 units, no drinking water, horse facilities, elev. 4200'.
Southwest of Mitchell. US Highway 26 southwest approximately 20 miles, FSR 22 to northeast edge of Big Summit Prairie and campground.

BARNHOUSE (Ochoco National Forest)
5 units, trailers to 22', no drinking water.
Southeast of Mitchell. US Highway 26 east 13.0 miles, FSR 12 south 5.0 miles, campground is at the summit of Ochoco Pass.

SCOTTS CAMP (Ochoco National Forest)
3 units, spring, elev. 4100'.
Southwest of Mitchell. US Highway 26 southwest approximately 20 miles, FSR 22 for 6.0 miles to junction with FSR 2630 and campground.

MT. VERNON (E-10)

BILLY FIELDS (Malheur National Forest)
6 units, trailers to 22', stream, fishing, picnic area, near Cedar Grove Botanical Area, elev. 4000'.
Southwest of Mt. Vernon. US Highway 26 west 10.0 miles, FSR 21 south 7.0 miles.

MAGONE LAKE (Malheur National Forest)
25 units, some trailers to 18', picnic area, piped water, lake - speed limits, boat launch, boating, fishing, swimming, hiking trails, elev. 5000'.
Northeast of Mt. Vernon. US Highway 395 north 9.0 miles, FSR 36 northeast 8.0 miles, FSR 3620 north 1.5 miles, FSR 3618 west 1.0 mile.

OREGON MINE CAMPGROUND (Malheur National Forest)
6 units, trailers to 22', stream, fishing, elev. 4300'.
Southwest of Mt. Vernon. US Highway 26 west 10.0 miles, FSR 21 south 14.0 miles, FSR 2170 northwest 1.0 mile.

MYRTLE POINT (A-11)

BENNETT PARK (Coos County)
18 units, pit toilets, picnic area, fishing, hiking.
Northeast of Myrtle Point. Dora-Sitkum Highway northeast 8.0 miles. Campground is near Gravel Ford.

CHERRY CREEK PARK (Coos County)
11 units, picnic facilities & shelter, pit toilets, spring water, fishing.
Northeast of Myrtle Point. Dora-Sitkum Highway northeast 16.5 miles, Dora Road north 2.5 miles.

FRONA PARK (Coos County)
17 units, picnic facilities, spring water, pit toilets, fishing.
Northeast of Myrtle Point. Dora-Sitkum Highway northeast 18.0 miles.

OAKRIDGE (C-10)

BLAIR LAKE (Willamette National Forest)
9 units, some hike-in sites, well, lake - no motors, fishing, swimming, hiking, elev. 4800'.

Northeast of Oakridge. CR 149 east 1.0 mile, FSR 24 northeast 8.0 miles, FSR 1934 northeast 7.4 miles, FSR 733 east 1.5 miles.

CAMPERS FLAT (Willamette National Forest)
5 units, trailers to 22', well, river, fishing, hiking, elev. 2000'.
Southeast of Oakridge. State Highway 58 southeast 2.2 miles, CR 360 southeast .5 mile, FSR 21 south 20.0 miles.

FERRIN (Willamette National Forest)
7 units, trailers to 18', river, fishing, elev. 1200'.
West of Oakridge. State Highway 58 west 2.1 miles.

HARRALSON HORSE CAMP (Willamette National Forest)
5 units, trailers to 18', trailer waste disposal, boat launch, boating, swimming, fishing, access to Waldo Lake Recreation Area, elev. 5500'.
East of Oakridge. State Highway 58 southeast 23.1 miles, FSR 5897 northeast 10.5 miles, FSR 5898 northwest 1.3 miles.

INDIGO LAKE (Willamette National Forest)
5 units, hike-in only, lake, swimming, fishing, dispersed camping, elev. 5900'.
Southeast of Oakridge. State Highway 58 southeast 2.2 miles, CR 360 southeast .5 mile, FSR 21 southeast 38.4 miles, FSR 2154 south 3.2 miles, Trail #3649 south 2.0 miles.

INDIGO SPRINGS (Willamette National Forest)
3 units, trailers to 18', creek, elev. 2800'.
Southeast of Oakridge. State Highway 58 southeast 2.2 miles, CR 360 southeast .5 mile, FSR 21 southeast 28.8 miles.

OPAL LAKE (Willamette National Forest)
1 walk-in tent unit, lake - no motors, carry-in boating, fishing, nearby trails, elev. 5400'.
Southeast of Oakridge. State Highway 58 southeast 2.2 miles, CR 360 southeast .5 mile, FSR 21 southeast 38.4 miles, FSR 2154 south 2.1 miles, hike-in .2 mile.

RHODODENDRON ISLAND (Willamette National Forest)
3 tent units, boat-in only, lake - speed limits, boating, swimming, fishing, elev. 5400'.
Southeast of Oakridge. State Highway 58 southeast 23.1 miles, FSR 5897 northeast 6.2 miles, FSR 5896 northwest 2.5 miles, boat northwest 1.6 miles to island campground.

SACANDAGA (Willamette National Forest)
19 units, trailers okay, fishing, hiking, elev. 2400'.
Southeast of Oakridge. State Highway 58 southeast 2.2 miles, CR 360 southeast .5 mile, FSR 21 southeast 23.3 miles.

SECRET (Willamette National Forest)
6 units, trailers to 18', river, fishing, elev. 2000'.
Southeast of Oakridge. State Highway 58 southeast 2.2 miles, CR 360 southeast .5 mile, FSR 21 south 18.3 miles.

TIMPANOGAS LAKE (Willamette National Forest)
10 units, trailers to 22', well, lake - no motors, swimming, fishing, trails, elev. 5200'.
Southeast of Oakridge. State Highway 58 southeast 2.2 miles, CR 360 southeast .5 mile, FSR 21 southeast 38.4 miles, FSR 2154 south 3.0 miles.

OXBOW (F-8)

DOVE CREEK (Wallowa-Whitman National Forest)
4 tent units, hike-in only, piped water, fishing, elev. 1700'.
North of Oxbow. CR 210 north 8.0 miles, Trail #1890 north 6.5 miles.

KIRBY CREEK (Wallowa-Whitman National Forest)
4 tent units, hike-in only, piped water, boating, swimming, fishing, water skiing, elev. 1700'.
North of Oxbow. CR 210 north 8.0 miles, Trail #1890 north 6.4 miles.

LEEP CREEK (Wallowa-Whitman National Forest)
3 tent units, hike-in only, picnic area, lake, boating, swimming, fishing, water skiing, elev. 1700'.
North of Oxbow. CR 210 north 8.0 miles, Trail #1890 north 4.7 miles.

LYNCH CREEK (Wallowa-Whitman National Forest)
3 tent units, hike-in only, picnic area, lake, boating, swimming, fishing, water skiing, elev. 1700'.
North of Oxbow. CR 210 north 8.0 miles, Trail #1890 north 7.3 miles.

VERMILLION BAR (Wallowa-Whitman National Forest)
2 tent units, hike-in only, picnic area, lake, boating, swimming, fishing, water skiing, elev. 1700'.
North of Oxbow. CR 210 north 8.0 miles, Trail #1890 north 6.9 miles.

PAISLEY (D-11)

CAMPBELL LAKE (Fremont National Forest)
15 units, trailers to 22', well, picnic area, high mountain lake - electric motors only, hiking, boat ramp, elev. 7200'.
Southwest of Paisley. CR 2-8 west 1.0 mile, FSR 3315 west 22.7 miles, FSR 28 south 3.0 miles, FSR 280033 west 3.4 miles.

DAIRY POINT (Fremont National Forest)
4 units, trailers to 30', stream, fishing, elev. 5200'.
Southwest of Paisley. CR 2-8 west 1.0 mile, FSR 33 south 20.3 miles, FSR 28 south 2.0 miles. Also accessible from Lakeview.

DEADHORSE LAKE (Fremont National Forest)
14 units, 11 group sites, trailers to 22', well, high mountain lake - electric motors only, boating, boat ramp, fishing, hiking, elev. 7400'.
Southwest of Paisley. CR 2-8 west 1.0 mile, FSR 3315 west 22.7 miles, FSR 28 south 3.0 miles, FSR 280033 west 4.4 miles.

HAPPY CAMP (Fremont National Forest)
9 units, trailers to 18', piped water, on Dairy Creek, good fishing, elev. 5200'.
Southwest of Paisley. CR 2-8 west 1.0 mile, FSR 33 south 20.3 miles, FSR 28 south 2.4 miles, FSR 280047 west 2.5 miles.

LEE THOMAS (Fremont National Forest)
7 units, trailers to 22', well, river, nearby fishing, hiking, remote, elev. 6200'.
Southwest of Paisley. CR 2-8 west 1.0 mile, FSR 33 south 7.1 miles.

PIKES CROSSING (Fremont National Forest)
6 units, trailers to 32', river, fishing, remote, elev. 5660'.
West of Paisley. State Highway 31 west 10.0 miles, FSR 29 west 12.0 miles, FSR 28 west 3.0 miles, FSR 30 west 3.0 miles.

SANDHILL CROSSING (Fremont National Forest)
5 units, trailers to 18', well, river, good fishing, hiking, remote, elev. 6100'.
Southwest of Paisley. CR 2-8 west 1.0 mile, FSR 3315 west 22.7 miles, FSR 28 south 1.0 mile, FSR 3411 west 6.0 miles.

PARKDALE (C-8)

CLOUD CAP SADDLE (Mt. Hood National Forest)
3 tent units, piped water, starting point for climbing Mt. Hood or hiking Timberline Trail, historic area, elev. 5900'.
Southwest of Parkdale. State Highway 35 south 8.0 miles, FSR 3512 west 11.7 miles.

GIBSON PRAIRIE HORSE CAMP (Mt. Hood National Forest)
4 units, trailers to 18', trails, elev. 3900'.
Northeast of Parkdale. State Highway 35 north 3.0 miles, FSR 17 southeast 15.0 miles.

HOOD RIVER MEADOWS TRAILHEAD (Mt. Hood National Forest)
3 tent units, stream, fishing, trailhead to Mt. Hood Wilderness, elev. 4400'.
Southwest of Parkdale. State Highway 35 southeast 25.0 miles.

INDIAN SPRINGS (Mt. Hood National Forest)
4 tent units, stream, trails, access to Pacific Crest Trail, elev. 4200'.

Northwest of Parkdale. State Highway 281 north 6.0 miles, CR 422 southwest 5.0 miles, FSR 13 west 5.0 miles, FSR 1310 northwest 10.5 miles.

KINNIKINNICK LAURANCE LAKE (Hood River County)
8 campsites, no water, lake - no gas motors, fishing, boating.
South of Parkdale. Clear Creek Road 10.0 miles to Laurance Lake and campground.

RAINY LAKE (Mt. Hood National Forest)
4 tent units, boating, swimming, fishing, trails, elev. 4100'.
Northwest of Parkdale. State Highway 281 north 6.0 miles, FSR 18 west 2.0 miles, FSR 2820 northwest 5.0 miles, FSR 28206 west 3.0 miles. Lake is .1 mile from campground.

TILLY JANE (Mt. Hood National Forest)
14 units, hike-in only, stream, trails, historic area, elev. 5700'.
Southwest of Parkdale. State Highway 35 south 8.0 miles, FSR 3512 west 11.7 miles.

WAHTUM LAKE (Mt. Hood National Forest)
5 units, trailers to 18', hike-in to lake and 8 more tent sites, boating, swimming, fishing, trails, elev. 3900'.
Northwest of Parkdale. State Highway 281 north 6.0 miles, CR 422 southwest 5.0 miles, FSR 13 west 5.0 miles, FSR 1310 northwest 8.0 miles. Located .3 mile from lake; trail to additional tent units and lake.

PAULINA (D-10)

BIG SPRING (Ochoco National Forest)
2 units, piped water, primitive, elev. 5000'.
South of Paulina. CR 112 east 3.5 miles, CR 113 north 6.5 miles, FSR 42 northwest 14.0 miles, FSR 4270 north 2.0 miles.

FRAZIER (Ochoco National Forest)
5 units, trailers to 22', fishing, bicycle path, primitive, elev. 5000'.

Northeast of Paulina. CR 112 east 3.5 miles, CR 113 north
2.2 miles, CR 135 east 10.0 miles, FSR 58 east 6.3 miles,
FSR 1548 northeast 1.1 miles.

MUD SPRING (Ochoco National Forest)
4 units, trailers to 22', no water, elev. 5000'.
Northeast of Paulina. CR 112 east 3.5 miles, CR 113 north
2.2 miles, CR 135 east 10.0 miles, FSR 58 east 4.2 miles,
FSR 5840 north 6.0 miles.

PENDLETON (E-7)

UMATILLA FORKS (Umatilla National Forest)
15 units, some trailers to 22', piped water, access to North
Forks Umatilla Wilderness, river, fishing, hiking, horse
trails, elev. 2400'
East of Pendleton. CR N32 east 32.0 miles, FSR 32
southeast .6 mile.

PORT ORFORD (A-11)

BUTLER BAR (Siskiyou National Forest)
16 units, trailers to 18', river, swimming, fishing, elev.
600'.
East of Port Orford. US Highway 101 north 3.0 miles, CR
208 southeast 7.4 miles, FSR 5325 southeast 11.2 miles.

ELK LAKE (Siskiyou National Forest)
3 units, trailers to 18', lake - no floating devices allowed,
swimming, fishing, elev. 1800'.
East of Port Orford. US Highway 101 north 3.0 miles, CR
208 southeast 7.4 miles, FSR 5325 southeast 16.7 miles.

POWERS (A-11)

MYRTLE GROVE (Siskiyou National Forest)
4 tent units, river, swimming, fishing, hiking, primitive,
elev. 600'.
Southeast of Powers. CR 90 southeast 4.2 miles, FSR
3300 south 4.5 miles.

ROCK CREEK (Siskiyou National Forest)
6 units, no trailers, swimming, fishing, trails, primitive, elev. 1200'.
South of Powers. CR 90 southeast 4.2 miles, FSR 3300 south 13.0 miles, FSR 3347 southwest 1.3 miles.

SQUAW LAKE (Siskiyou National Forest)
7 units, lake - no floating devices, swimming, fishing, trails, primitive, elev. 2200'.
Southeast of Powers. CR 90 southeast 4.2 miles, FSR 3300 south 12.6 miles, FSR 321 southeast 4.6 miles, FSR 3342 east 1.0 mile.

PRAIRIE CITY (E-9)

CRESCENT (Malheur National Forest)
4 units, trailers to 18', stream, fishing, elev. 5200'.
Southeast of Prairie City. CR 14 southeast 8.3 miles, FSR 14 south 8.5 miles.

DIXIE (Malheur National Forest)
11 units, trailers to 22', well, picnic area, berry picking, elev. 5000'.
Northeast of Prairie City. US Highway 26 northeast 7.0 miles, FSR 848 north .5 mile.

ELK CREEK (Malheur National Forest)
5 units, trailers to 22', no water, stream, fishing, adjacent to N. Fork Malheur River, hiking, elev. 5000'.
Southeast of Prairie City. CR 62 southeast 8.3 miles, FSR 13 southeast 16.0 miles, FSR 16 south 1.3 miles.

INDIAN SPRINGS (Malheur National Forest)
10 tent units, primitive, hiking trails, stream, wilderness access, 6000'.
South of Prairie City. CR 62 south 11.0 miles, FSR 14 southeast 11.0 miles, FSR 16 west 11.3 miles, FSR 1640 north 6.5 miles.

LITTLE CRANE (Malheur National Forest)
5 units, trailers to 32', stream, fishing, hiking trail, elev. 5500'.

Southeast of Prairie City. CR 14 southeast 8.3 miles, FSR
13 south 16.0 miles, FSR 16 south 5.7 miles.

McNAUGHTON SPRING (Malheur National Forest)
4 units, trailers to 22', stream, fishing, wilderness access,
elev. 4800'.
South of Prairie City. CR 60 south 8.7 miles, FSR 6001
south .3 mile.

NORTH FORK MALHEUR (Malheur National Forest)
5 units, trailers okay, on N. Fork Malheur River, fishing,
hiking, elev. 4700'.
Southeast of Prairie City. CR 62 southeast 8.3 miles, FSR
13 southeast 16.0 miles, FSR 16 south 2.0 miles, FSR
1675 south 2.7 miles.

SLIDE CREEK (Malheur National Forest)
1 group site, trailers to 22', stream, fishing, hiking,
wilderness access, horse corral, elev. 4900'.
South of Prairie City. CR 60 south 8.7 miles, FSR 6001
south .6 mile.

STRAWBERRY (Malheur National Forest)
11 units, trailers to 22', piped water, stream, boating,
fishing, trailhead to Strawberry Mountain Wilderness,
horse corrals, elev. 5700'.
South of Prairie City. CR 60 south 8.7 miles, FSR 6001
south 2.3 miles.

TROUT FARM (Malheur National Forest)
9 units, trailers to 22', picnic shelter, piped water, small
fishing pond, hiking, elev. 4900'.
Southeast of Prairie City. CR 14 southeast 8.3 miles, FSR
14 south 6.9 miles. Rough road.

PRINEVILLE (E-10)

DEEP CREEK (Ochoco National Forest)
6 units, trailers to 22', piped water, fishing, elev. 4200'.
East of Prineville. US 26 east 16.7 miles, CR 123 northeast
8.5 miles, FSR 42 southeast 23.6 miles, FSR 460 south .1
mile.

ELKHORN (Ochoco National Forest)
4 units, trailers to 32', piped water, primitive, elev. 4500'.
Southeast of Prineville. CR 380 southeast 34.0 miles, FSR 16 southeast 4.3 miles.

OCHOCO (Ochoco National Forest)
6 units, water, creek, hiking trails, picnic grounds, elev. 4000'.
East of Prineville. US Highway 26 east 18.0 miles, FSR 22 for 8.5 miles. Located at junction with FSR 2610, adjacent to Ochoco Ranger Station.

WILDWOOD (Ochoco National Forest)
5 units, trailers to 22', water, primitive, elev. 4800'.
Northeast of Prineville. US Highway 26 east 27.0 miles, FSR 2630 east 3.0 miles, FSR 2210 north 3.0 miles.

WILEY FLAT (Ochoco National Forest)
5 campsites, trailers to 32', piped water, primitive, elev. 5000'.
Southeast of Prineville. CR 380 southeast 34.0 miles, FSR 16 southeast 9.8 miles, FSR 16 west 1.0 mile.

PROSPECT (C-11)

HUCKLEBERRY (Rogue River National Forest)
15 units, trailers to 22', well, berry picking, elev. 5400'.
Northeast of Prospect. State Highway 62 east 17.4 miles, FSR 60 south 4.1 miles.

MILL CREEK (Rogue River National Forest)
8 units, trailers to 22', fishing, elev. 2800'.
North of Prospect. State Highway 62 north 2.0 miles, FSR 30 east 1.0 mile.

NATURAL BRIDGE (Rogue River National Forest)
16 units, trailers to 22', river, fishing, trails, river flows underground here, elev. 3200'.
North of Prospect. State Highway 62 north 9.9 miles, FSR 30 west 1.0 mile.

RIVER BRIDGE (Rogue River National Forest)
6 units, trailers to 22', river, fishing, hiking, elev. 2900'.

North of Prospect. State Highway 62 north 4.0 miles, FSR 6210 north 1.0 mile.

REMOTE (A-11)

BEAR CREEK (BLM)
17 units, no water, elev. 700'.
East of Remote. State Highway 42 east 8.0 miles.

RICHLAND (F-9)

EAGLE CREEK (Wallowa-Whitman National Forest)
10 units, trailers to 22', stream, fishing, elev. 3400'.
Northwest of Richland. CR 833 northwest 8.1 miles, FSR 7735 northwest 14.0 miles, FSR 7700 northwest 7.0 miles.

EAGLE FORKS (Wallowa-Whitman National Forest)
7 units, trailers to 18', picnic area, piped water, stream, fishing, elev. 4000'.
Northwest of Richland. CR 833 northwest 8.1 miles, FSR 7735 north 2.7 miles.

SWEDES LANDING (BLM)
Campsites, restrooms, boat ramp, Brownlee Reservoir.
Southeast of Richland. Brownlee Reservoir Road southeast 14.0 miles.

TUNNEL LAUNCH (BLM)
Campsites, boat ramp, Brownlee Reservoir.
Northeast of Richland. Brownlee Reservoir Road northeast 34.0 miles to campground.

ROGUE RIVER (B-12)

ELDERBERRY FLAT (BLM)
10 campsites, elev. 2000'.
North of Rogue River. Take the road to Wimer, after 19.0 miles you'll find the campground on the left.

ROME (F-11)

ROME CAMPGROUND (BLM)
6 units, drinking water, boat ramp, elev. 3400'.
At Rome. Located at Rome; adjacent to Owyhee River.

SCAPPOOSE (B-7)

SCAPONIA (Columbia County)
7 units, drinking water, stream, elev. 600'.
Northwest of Scappoose. Campground is 18.0 miles northwest of Scappoose along the road leading to Vernonia/Pittsburgh.

SELMA (A-12)

ONION CAMP (Siskiyou National Forest)
3 units, hiking, fishing, wilderness trailhead, primitive.
West of Selma. Campground is located 17 miles west of Selma.

SENECA (E-10)

BIG CREEK (Malheur National Forest)
14 units, trailers to 22', well, stream, fishing, elev. 5100'.
East of Seneca. FSR 16 east 20.5 miles, FSR 815 north .5 mile; campground is on edge of Logan Valley.

MURRAY (Malheur National Forest)
5 units, trailers to 22', stream, fishing, hiking, elev. 5200'.
East of Seneca. FSR 16 east 19.0 miles, FSR 934 north 2.0 miles. Campground is located 5 miles from Strawberry Mountain Wilderness.

PARISH CABIN (Malheur National Forest)
17 units, 3 group sites, trailers to 22', picnic area, piped water, stream, fishing, elev. 4900'.
East of Seneca. FSR 16 east 12.0 miles.

STARR (Malheur National Forest)
8 units, trailers to 18', no water, picnic area, elev. 5100'.
North of Seneca. US Highway 395 north 9.1 miles.

SILVER LAKE (D-11)

DUNCAN RESERVOIR (BLM)
5 units, picnic area, boat ramp, year round, elev. 4800'.
Southeast of Silver Lake. Duncan Reservoir Road southeast 8.0 miles.

EAST BAY (Fremont National Forest)
17 units, trailers to 32', well, lake - speed limits, boat ramp, boating, swimming, fishing, elev. 5000'.
South of Silver Lake. State Highway 31 west .5 mile, CR 4-12 south 5.0 miles, FSR 28 south 7.5 miles, FSR 280014 west 1.5 miles.

SILVER CREEK MARSH (Fremont National Forest)
7 units, trailers to 22', picnic area, well, stream, fishing, elev. 5000'.
Southwest of Silver Lake. State Highway 31 west 1.0 mile, CR 4-11 south 5.5 miles, FSR 27 south 4.0 miles.

THOMPSON RESERVOIR (Fremont National Forest)
19 units, trailers to 22', well, lake - speed limits, boating, swimming, boat ramp, good fishing, elev. 5000'.
South of Silver Lake. State Highway 31 west 1.0 mile, CR 4-11 south 5.5 miles, FSR 27 south 7.0 miles, FSR 270021 east 1.1 miles.

SISTERS (D-10)

BIG LAKE WEST (Willamette National Forest)
12 tent units, walk-in sites, boating, swimming, fishing, water skiing, hiking trails, elev. 4600'.
West of Sisters. US Highway 20 west 21.7 miles, FSR 2690 south 4.3 miles; campground is on the west shore of Big Lake.

BLACK PINE SPRINGS (Deschutes National Forest)
9 units, trailers to 18', elev. 4300'.
South of Sisters. FSR 16 south 9.0 miles.

DRIFTWOOD (Deschutes National Forest)
20 units, trailers to 18', lake - no motors, boating, swimming, fishing, trails, elev. 6400'.

South of Sisters. FSR 16 south 18.0 miles, campground road south 1.0 mile.

GRAHAM CORRAL (Deschutes National Forest)
10 units, trailers to 18', piped water, trails, horse facilities, elev. 3400'.
Northwest of Sisters. US Highway 20 northwest 4.5 miles, FSR 1012 southwest 1.0 mile. FSR 300 northwest .8 mile, FSR 340 northwest 1.0 mile.

LAVA CAMP LAKE (Deschutes National Forest)
12 units, trailers to 22', swimming, fishing, trails, elev. 5300'.
West of Sisters. State Highway 242 west 13.0 miles; located .2 mile off highway.

ROUND LAKE (Deschutes National Forest)
5 tent units, lake - no motors, boat launch, boating, swimming, fishing, elev. 4200'.
Northwest of Sisters. US Highway 20 northwest 12.0 miles, FSR 12 north 1.0 mile, FSR 1210 northwest 5.0 miles.

THREE CREEK LAKE (Deschutes National Forest)
10 units, trailers to 18', lake - no motors, boating, swimming, fishing, elev. 6400'.
South of Sisters. FSR 16 south 15.0 miles.

THREE CREEK MEADOW (Deschutes National Forest)
19 units, 10 group sites, trailers to 18', creek, trails, horse facilities, elev. 6300'.
South of Sisters. CR 16 south 14.0 miles.

WHISPERING PINE (Deschutes National Forest)
8 units, trailers to 22', creek, fishing, elev. 4400'.
Southwest of Sisters. State Highway 242 west 5.5 miles, FSR 1018 south 3.0 miles.

SIXES (A-11)

SIXES RIVER (BLM)
19 units, trails, elev. 400'.
East of Sixes. Head east along river for 11.0 miles.

SPRAY (D-9)

FAIRVIEW (Umatilla National Forest)
5 units, trailers to 18', no water, elev. 4100'.
Northeast of Spray. State Highway 19 east 2.5 miles, State Highway 207 north 11.5 miles, FSR 400 west .5 mile.

MULESHOE (BLM)
11 units, picnic area, boat ramp, swimming area, year round, elev. 600'.
West of Spray. State Highway 207 west, campground is located adjacent to John Day River between Spray and Service Creek.

STEAMBOAT (B-11)

APPLE CREEK (Umpqua National Forest)
8 units, trailers to 22', on N. Umpqua River, no drinking water, fly fishing, hiking, elev. 1365'.
East of Steamboat. State Highway 138 east 4.9 miles.

BOULDER FLAT (Umpqua National Forest)
10 units, trailers to 22', 1 group site, on N. Umpqua River, no drinking water, picnic facilities, white water boating, fly fishing, hiking, adjacent to Boulder Creek Wilderness, elev. 1600'.
East of Steamboat. State Highway 138 east 14.1 miles.

BUNKER HILL (Umpqua National Forest)
8 units, trailers to 18', on Lemolo Lake, boating, no drinking water, picnic facilities, swimming, fishing, water skiing, elev. 4200'.
East of Steamboat. State Highway 138 east 31.4 miles, Lemolo Lake Road north 5.4 miles, cross dam and turn right onto FSR 2610/999. Campground is .5 mile southeast on north shore of lake.

CALAMUT LAKE (Umpqua National Forest)
1 tent unit, hike-in only, lake - no motors, swimming, fishing, primitive, elev. 5900'.
Northeast of Steamboat. State Highway 138 east 36.3 miles, FSR 2500 northeast 7.2 miles, FSR 2165 northwest 2.0 miles, Trail #1494 north 1.2 miles.

CLEARWATER FALLS (Umpqua National Forest)
5 units, trailers to 18', picnic facilities, no water, waterfall, fishing, elev. 4200'.
East of Steamboat. State Highway 138 east 28.2 miles.

EAST LEMOLO (Umpqua National Forest)
Campsites, trailers to 22', picnic facilities, primitive fishing camp, at Lemolo Lake, boating, swimming, water skiing, elev. 4200'.
Northeast of Steamboat. State Highway 138 east 31.4 miles, Lemolo Lake Road north 3.2 miles, FSR 400 northeast 2.3 miles.

INLET (Umpqua National Forest)
14 units, trailers to 22', river, picnic facilities, no drinking water, water skiing, elev. 4200'.
East of Steamboat. State Highway 138 east 31.4 miles, Lemolo Lake Road north 3.2 miles, FSR 400 northeast 2.7 miles. Located on Lemolo Lake at confluence of North Umpqua River.

ISLAND (Umpqua National Forest)
7 units, trailers to 22', picnic facilities, no drinking water, N. Umpqua River, fly fishing, hiking, white water rafting, elev. 1189'.
East of Steamboat. State Highway 138 east 1.3 miles.

KELSAY VALLEY (Umpqua National Forest)
2 units, trailers to 18', no drinking water, picnic facilities, stream, fishing, horse camping, trails, primitive, elev. 4300'.
East of Steamboat. State Highway 138 east 32.4 miles, Windigo Pass Road northeast 4.7 miles, Kelsay Valley Road east .3 mile. Near Lemolo Lake.

LEMOLO TWO FOREBAY (Umpqua National Forest)
4 units, trailers to 18', lake, no tables, swimming, fishing, primitive, elev. 3200'.
East of Steamboat. State Highway 138 east 17.2 miles, FSR 34 northeast 3.9 miles, FSR 3402 west 1.2 miles.

SCARED MAN (BLM)
10 units, no water, river, swimming, elev. 1300'.

North of Steamboat. Camton County Road 4.0 miles to campground.

STEAMBOAT FALLS (Umpqua National Forest)
11 units, some trailers to 24', no drinking water, stream - no fishing, swimming, hiking, elev. 1400'.
Northeast of Steamboat. CR 38 northeast 5.5 miles, FSR 3810 southeast .6 mile.

THIELSEN (Umpqua National Forest)
3 tent units, stream, elev. 4400'.
East of Steamboat. State Highway 138 east 32.1 miles.

TOKETEE LAKE (Umpqua National Forest)
33 units, trailers to 22', picnic facilities, no water, river, boat launch, fishing, water skiing, on northeast end of Toketee Lake, elev. 2400'.
East of Steamboat. State Highway 138 east 17.2 miles, FSR 34 northeast 1.4 miles.

TWIN LAKES (Umpqua National Forest)
6 tent units, shelter, hike-in only, lake - no motors, boating, swimming, fishing, primitive, trails, elev. 5000'.
East of Steamboat. State Highway 138 east 11.9 miles, FSR 4770 southeast 10.0 miles, Trail #1500 west 1.1 miles.

WHITEHORSE FALLS (Umpqua National Forest)
5 units, trailers to 18', no drinking water, picnic area, stream, waterfall, fishing, next to Clearwater River, elev. 3800'.
East of Steamboat. State Highway 138 east 24.4 miles.

SUMPTER (E-9)

DEER CREEK (Wallowa-Whitman National Forest)
8 tent units, picnic area, fishing, primitive, elev. 4600'.
Northeast of Sumpter. State Highway 410 southeast 4.0 miles, State Highway 7 southeast 5.0 miles, FSR 6550 north 3.0 miles.

McCULLY FORKS (Wallowa-Whitman National Forest)
5 units, 2 group sites, stream, fishing, elev. 4600'.

Northwest of Sumpter. State Highway 410 northwest 3.0 miles to campground.

MILLERS LAND (Wallowa-Whitman National Forest)
7 units, trailers to 18', lake, boating, swimming, fishing, water skiing, elev. 4100'.
Southeast of Sumpter. State Highway 410 southeast 4.0 miles, State Highway 7 southeast 6.0 miles, CR 667 south 2.0 miles, FSR 2220 southeast 2.0 miles.

SOUTHWEST OVERFLOW (Wallowa-Whitman National Forest)
18 units, trailers to 18', Phillips Lake, swimming, fishing, water skiing, boat launch, elev. 4100'.
Southeast of Sumpter. State Highway 410 southeast 4.0 miles, State Highway 7 southeast 5.0 miles, FSR 2220 southeast 2.6 miles.

SUNRIVER (D-10)

BESSON CAMP (Deschutes National Forest)
5 units, trailers okay, on Deschutes River, boat launch, primitive.
Near Sunriver. Leave US Highway 97 at Sunriver's main exit and keep to the left as you approach Sunriver exit. Cross Harper Bridge, turn right on FSR 41 and go .2 mile north to FSR 200 which will take you .8 mile east to campground.

TAFT (A-9)

NORTH CREEK (Siuslaw National Forest)
11 units, swimming, fishing, stream, primitive, elev. 400'.
Southeast of Taft. US 101 south 3.1 miles, State Highway 229 southeast 5.1 miles, FSR 727 north 5.3 miles.

TILLER (B-11)

BOULDER CREEK & ANNEX (Umpqua National Forest)
12 units, trailers to 18', well, creek, hiking, elev. 1400'.
Northeast of Tiller. State Highway 227 southeast .3 mile, S. Umpqua Road #28 northeast 14.0 miles.

BUNCH GRASS MEADOWS (Umpqua National Forest)
Campsite/shelter, elev. 4000'.
East of Tiller. State Highway 227 southeast .3 mile, S. Umpqua Road #28 northeast 5.0 miles, FSR 293 east 3.7 miles, FSR 300 south .7 mile, FSR 3014 for 2.5 miles, FSR 3034 south 3.0 miles.

CAMP COMFORT (Umpqua National Forest)
5 units, 1 shelter, trailers to 18', picnic facilities, stream, fishing, trails, elev. 2000'.
Northeast of Tiller. State Highway 227 southeast .3 mile, S. Umpqua Road #28 northeast 26.0 miles.

COVER (Umpqua National Forest)
7 units, trailers to 18', stream, fishing, hiking, elev. 1700'.
Northeast of Tiller. State Highway 227 southeast .3 mile, S. Umpqua Road #28 northeast 5.0 miles, Jackson Creek Road east 13.0 miles.

DUMONT CREEK (Umpqua National Forest)
5 units, trailers to 18', picnic facilities, stream, fishing, elev. 1300'.
Northeast of Tiller. State Highway 227 southeast .3 mile, S. Umpqua Road #28 northeast 11.0 miles.

MUD LAKE (Umpqua National Forest)
1 tent unit/shelter, elev. 4800'.
Northeast of Tiller. State Highway 227 southeast .3 mile, S. Umpqua Road #28 northeast 6.2 miles, FSR 28 northeast 29.2 miles, FSR 2715 northwest 1.1 miles.

ROCKY RIDGE (Umpqua National Forest)
1 tent unit/shelter, trails, elev. 5500'.
Northeast of Tiller. State Highway 227 southeast .3 mile, S. Umpqua Road #28 northeast 6.2 miles, FSR 284 northeast 20.4 miles, FSR 2830 southeast 1.7 miles, FSR 2840 northeast 8.3 miles.

THREEHORN (Umpqua National Forest)
5 units, trailers to 22', picnic facilities, well, hiking, elev. 2600'.
South of Tiller. CR 1 south 13.0 miles.

WHISKEY CAMP (Umpqua National Forest)
2 tent units, primitive, trails, elev. 3800'.
Southeast of Tiller. State Highway 227 southeast .3 mile, S. Umpqua Road #28 northeast 5.0 miles, FSR 293 east 3.7 miles, FSR 300 south .7 mile, FSR 3014 southeast 8.7 miles.

TOLLGATE (E-7)

ALPINE SPRING (Umatilla National Forest)
3 tent units, no trailers, river, hiking, elev. 5000'.
Southeast of Tollgate. State Highway 204 to Balloon Tree Road N30, follow this to campground. Total distance from Tollgate 7.0 miles.

BEAR CANYON (Umatilla National Forest)
6 tent units, river, fishing, berry picking, hiking, elev. 4900'.
East of Tollgate. State Highway 204 to Eden Road N50, follow this to campground. Total distance from Tollgate 26.0 miles.

DEDUCK SPRINGS (Umatilla National Forest)
1 tent unit, picnic area, river, hiking, elev. 5600'.
Northeast of Tollgate. State Highway 204 east to Tiger Creek Road N-62, northeast to campground. Total distance from Tollgate 23.0 miles.

DUSTY SPRING (Umatilla National Forest)
5 tent units, piped water, picnic area, hiking, berry picking, elev. 5100'.
East of Tollgate. State Highway 204 east to Kendall-Skyline Road N910, east to campground. Total distance from Tollgate 9.0 miles.

ELK FLATS (Umatilla National Forest)
3 tent units, river, hiking, elev. 5000'.
East of Tollgate. State Highway 204 east to Eden Road N50, follow this to campground. Total distance from Tollgate 30.0 miles.

INDIAN (Umatilla National Forest)
2 tent units, picnic area, river, hiking, elev. 5800'.

Northeast of Tollgate. State Highway 204 east to Kendall-Skyline Road N910, northeast to campground. Total distance from Tollgate 27.0 miles.

LUGER SPRING (Umatilla National Forest)
5 units, some trailers, piped water, picnic area, hiking, elev. 5000'.
East of Tollgate. State Highway 204 east to Mottet Meadows Road N40, follow this to campground. Total distance from Tollgate 17.0 miles.

MOSIER SPRING (Umatilla National Forest)
4 units, some trailers, piped water, picnic area, hiking, berry picking, elev. 4700'.
East of Tollgate. State Highway 204 east to Eden Road N50, follow this to campground. Total distance from Tollgate 35.0 miles.

SQUAW SPRINGS (Umatilla National Forest)
3 tent units, no trailers, elev. 4900'.
South of Tollgate. State Highway 204 east to Summit Road N31, follow this to campground. Total distance from Tollgate 12.0 miles.

SQUAW SPRINGS (Umatilla National Forest)
10 units, some trailers, picnic area, hiking, elev. 5000'.
Northeast of Tollgate. State Highway 204 east to Kendall-Skyline Road N910, northeast to campground. Total distance from Tollgate 20.0 miles.

TIMOTHY SPRING (Umatilla National Forest)
8 units, some trailers, piped water, picnic area, hiking, berry picking, elev. 4600'.
Northeast of Tollgate. State Highway 204 east to Timothy Spring Road N534, follow this to campground. Total distance from Tollgate 17.0 miles.

TYGH VALLEY (D-8)

LITTLE BADGER (Mt. Hood National Forest)
2 units, trailers to 18', stream, fishing, elev. 2200'.
Northwest of Tygh Valley. CR 213 west 3.0 miles, CR 241

west 4.5 miles, FSR 27 west 2.0 miles, FSR 2710 west .5 mile, FSR 130 west .2 mile.

UKIAH (E-8)

BEAR WALLOW CREEK (Umatilla National Forest)
6 units, picnic area, no water, fishing, short handicap accessible trail along stream, elev. 3900'.
Northeast of Ukiah. State Highway 244 northeast 11.0 miles.

BIG CREEK (Umatilla National Forest)
2 units, no water, fishing, hiking, elev. 5100'.
Southeast of Ukiah. Ukiah-Granite Road S522 southeast 23.0 miles.

DIVIDE WELL (Umatilla National Forest)
3 tent units, no water, bike trails, elev. 4700'.
West of Ukiah. US Highway 395 south to Jones Prairie Road N415, follow this to campground. Campground is 17.0 miles west of Ukiah.

DRIFT FENCE (Umatilla National Forest)
3 tent units, no water, elev. 4250'.
Southeast of Ukiah. Ukiah-Granite Road S522 southeast 8.0 miles.

FRAZIER (Umatilla National Forest)
32 units, no water, group picnic area, some trailers to 32', stream, fishing, elev. 4300'.
East of Ukiah. State Highway 244 east 18.1 miles, FSR 5226 south .5 mile, FSR 20 east .2 mile.

LANE CREEK (Umatilla National Forest)
4 units, no water, picnic area, some trailers to 32', fishing, elev. 3850'.
Northeast of Ukiah. State Highway 244 northeast 10.5 miles.

NORTH FORK JOHN DAY (Umatilla National Forest)
5 units, no water, trailers to 22', river, fishing, access to North Fork John Day Wilderness, elev. 5200'.
Southeast of Ukiah. FSR 52 southeast 38.5 miles.

WINOM CREEK TRAILHEAD (Umatilla National Forest)
2 units, 5 group sites, no water, trails, wilderness access, elev. 5000'.
Southeast of Ukiah. FSR 52 southeast 20.0 miles, FSR 52440 for .2 miles to campground.

UNION (F-8)

NORTH CATHERINE TRAILHEAD (Wallowa-Whitman National Forest)
5 units, trailers to 22', stream, fishing, hiking, elev. 4400'.
Southeast of Union. State Highway 203 southeast 10.0 miles, FSR 7785 northeast 6.5 miles.

UNITY (E-9)

ELDORADO (Wallowa-Whitman National Forest)
2 units, trailers to 18', picnic area, stream, fishing, elev. 4000'.
Southeast of Unity. US Highway 26 southeast 10.0 miles, FSR 1600 southwest 2.0 mile.

ELK CREEK (Wallowa-Whitman National Forest)
Campsites, creek, fishing, elev. 4500'.
Southwest of Unity. CR 600 southwest 6.0 miles, FSR 6005 southwest 2.0 miles.

LONG CREEK (Wallowa-Whitman National Forest)
2 units, trailers to 18', creek.
South of Unity. FSR 1680 south 9.0 miles.

MAMMOTH SPRINGS (Wallowa-Whitman National Forest)
3 units, trailers to 18', creek, fishing, elev. 4400'.
Southwest of Unity. CR 600 southwest 6.0 miles, FSR 6005 southwest 2.5 miles.

OREGON (Wallowa-Whitman National Forest)
8 units, trailers to 18', picnic area, piped water, hiking, elev. 5000'.
Northwest of Unity. US Highway 26 northwest 10.5 miles.

SOUTH FORK (Wallowa-Whitman National Forest)
29 units, trailers to 18', picnic area, piped water, stream, fishing, elev. 4400'.
Southwest of Unity. CR 600 southwest 6.0 miles, FSR 6005 southwest 1.0 mile.

STEVENS CREEK (Wallowa-Whitman National Forest)
Campsites, stream, fishing, trail, elev. 4500'.
Southwest of Unity. CR 600 southwest 6.0 miles, FSR 6005 southwest 1.5 miles.

WETMORE (Wallowa-Whitman National Forest)
10 units, trailers to 18', picnic area, piped water, wheelchair access includes trail, hiking, elev. 4400'.
Northwest of Unity. US Highway 26 northwest 8.2 miles.

YELLOW PINE (Wallowa-Whitman National Forest)
21 units, trailers to 18', picnic area, piped water, wheelchair access includes trails, trailer waste disposal, hiking, elev. 4500'.
Northwest of Unity. US Highway 26 northwest 9.2 miles.

VALE (F-10)

TWIN SPRINGS (BLM)
3 units, water, restrooms, picnic sites, elev. 3200'.
Southwest of Vale. US Highway 20 southwest 30.0 miles.

WALDPORT (A-10)

CANAL CREEK (Siuslaw National Forest)
Group campsites, trailers to 22', picnic area, well, narrow roads, elev. 200'.
Southeast of Waldport. State Highway 34 east 7.0 miles, FSR 3462 south 4.1 miles.

WALLOWA (F-7)

BOUNDARY (Wallowa-Whitman National Forest)
12 units, trailers to 18', creek, swimming, fishing, trailhead to wilderness area, primitive, elev. 3600'.
South of Wallowa. CR 515 south 5.0 miles, FSR 8250 south 1.9 miles.

WAMIC (C-8)

BADGER LAKE (Mt. Hood National Forest)
4 tent units, lake - no motors, boating, swimming, fishing, elev. 4400'.
Northwest of Wamic. CR 226 west 6.0 miles, FSR 48 southwest 10.0 miles, FSR 4860 northwest 7.0 miles, FSR 140 northwest 5.0 miles.

BONNEY CROSSING (Mt. Hood National Forest)
8 units, stream, boating, fishing, elev. 2200'.
Northwest of Wamic. CR 226 west 6.0 miles, FSR 48 west 1.0 mile, FSR 4810 west 2.0 miles, FSR 4811 northwest 1.2 miles, FSR 2710 northwest 1.7 miles.

BONNEY MEADOWS (Mt. Hood National Forest)
6 units, trailers to 22', stream, fishing, elev. 4800'.
Northwest of Wamic. CR 226 west 6.0 miles, FSR 48 southwest 14.0 miles, FSR 4890 north 2.0 miles, FSR 4891 north 4.0 miles.

BOULDER LAKE (Mt. Hood National Forest)
3 tent units, hike-in only, lake - no motors, boating, swimming, fishing, elev. 4600'.
Northwest of Wamic. CR 226 west 6.0 miles, FSR 48 southwest 11.5 miles, FSR 4880 north 6.0 miles, Trail #463 west .5 mile.

CAMP WINDY (Mt. Hood National Forest)
2 tent units, fishing, elev. 4800'.
Northwest of Wamic. CR 226 west 6.0 miles, FSR 48 southwest 10.0 miles, FSR 4860 northwest 9.2 miles.

FOREST CREEK (Mt. Hood National Forest)
9 units, trailers to 22', fishing, elev. 3000'.
Southwest of Wamic. CR 226 west 6.0 miles, FSR 48 southwest 12.6 miles, FSR 4885 southeast 1.0 mile, FSR 3530 south .2 mile.

JEAN LAKE (Mt. Hood National Forest)
3 tent units, lake - no motors, boating, swimming, fishing, elev. 4800'.

Northwest of Wamic. CR 226 west 6.0 miles, FSR 48 southwest 10.0 miles, FSR 4860 northwest 9.2 miles, FSR 3550 northeast 2.0 miles.

POST CAMP (Mt. Hood National Forest)
3 units, trailers to 22', picnic area, fishing, elev. 4000'.
Southwest of Wamic. CR 226 west 6.0 miles, FSR 48 southwest 10.0 miles, FSR 4860 northwest 1.7 miles, FSR 240 east .5 mile, FSR 4813 northwest .7 mile.

WESTFIR (C-10)

SKOOKUM CREEK (Willamette National Forest)
8 units, well, trails to high country lakes, horse facilities, elev. 4500'.
Northeast of Westfir. FSR 19 northeast 31.4 miles, FSR 1957 southeast 3.7 miles.

WESTON (E-7)

MOTTET (Umatilla National Forest)
7 units, trailers to 22', spring, hiking, primitive, elev. 5200'.
East of Weston. State Highway 204 east 17.5 miles, FSR 64 east 2.9 miles, FSR 6403 northeast 9.8 miles.

WOODLAND (Umatilla National Forest)
7 units, trailers okay, no drinking water, pit toilets, must pack out garbage, elev. 5200'.
Southeast of Weston. State Highway 204 southeast 23.0 miles.

WHITE CITY (C-12)

BEAVER DAM (Rogue River National Forest)
4 tent units, creek, fishing, elev. 4500'.
East of White City. State Highway 140 northeast 29.7 miles, FSR 37 south 6.5 miles. Campground is south of Fish Lake.

DALEY CREEK (Rogue River National Forest)
5 tent units, creek, fishing, elev. 4500'.
East of White City. State Highway 140 northeast 29.7 miles, FSR 37 south 6.0 miles. Campground is south of Fish Lake.

NORTH FORK (Rogue River National Forest)
7 units, trailers to 18', stream, fishing, elev. 4500'.
East of White City. State Highway 140 northeast 28.1 miles, FSR 3706 south 1.0 mile.

WHITNEY (E-9)

FOURTH CREEK (Wallowa-Whitman National Forest)
2 units, primitive, creek, trails.
South of Whitney. State Highway 7 to CR 507, campground is 4.0 miles south.

YACHATS (A-10)

TENMILE CREEK (Siuslaw National Forest)
6 units, trailers to 18', fishing, nature trail, primitive, elev. 400'.
Southeast of Yachats. US Highway 101 south 7.0 miles, FSR 56 east 5.6 miles.

LOOKING FOR A CAMPGROUND WITH SHOWERS?

A CAMPER'S GUIDE TO OREGON & WASHINGTON by KiKi Canniff details the region's 1500 improved campgrounds. It's perfect for campers who want showers, swimming pools, trailer waste disposals, hookups for electricity, water, sewer or other amenities when they camp.

WHERE TO FIND WASHINGTON'S FREE CAMPGROUNDS

WASHINGTON MAP

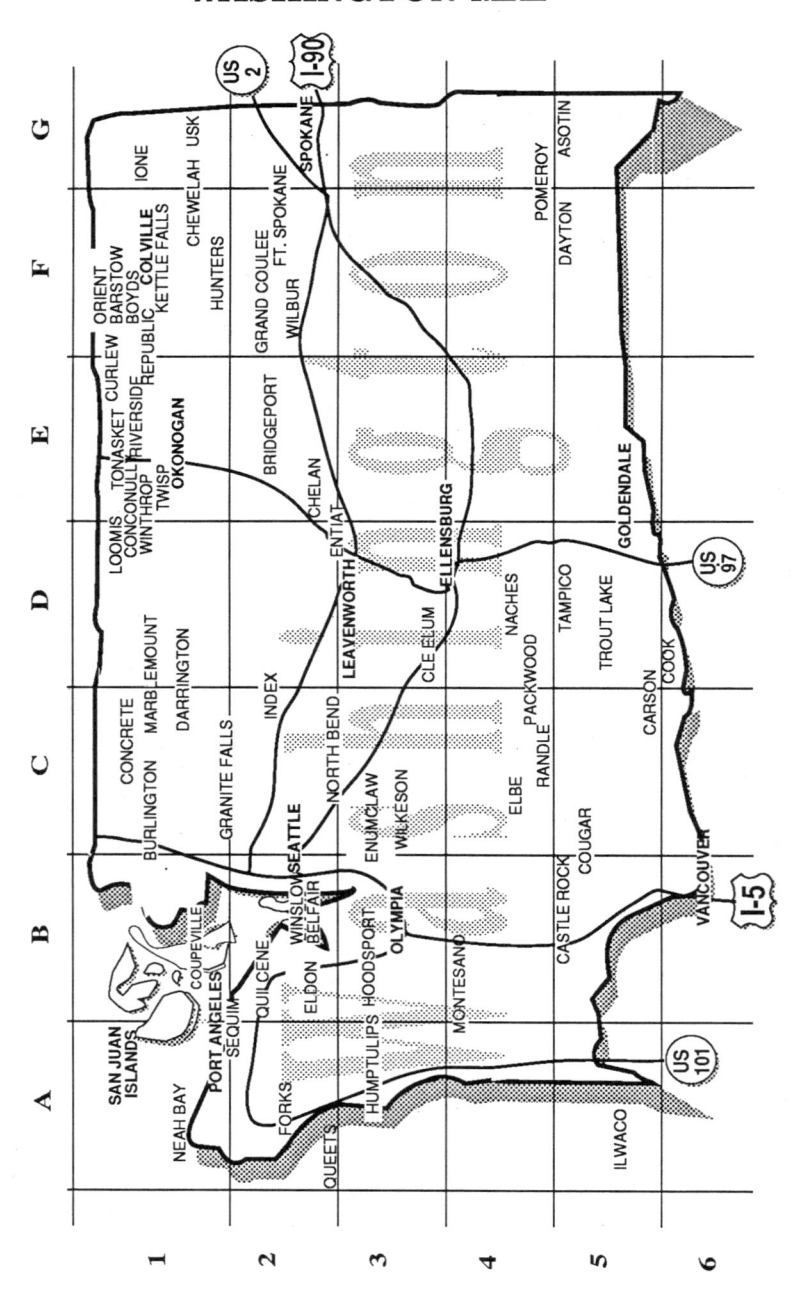

ASOTIN (G-5)

HELLER'S BAR (BLM)
10 units, boat ramp, restrooms, year round, Grande Ronde River, elev. 820'.
South of Asotin. State Highway 129 south 17.0 miles.

WICKIUP (Umatilla National Forest)
9 units, trailers to 18', no water, elev. 6000'.
Southwest of Asotin. CR 105 southwest 24.0 miles, FSR 4300 7.0 miles southwest.

BARSTOW (F-1)

ELBOW LAKE (Colville National Forest)
5 units, trailers to 18', elev. 3000'.
Northeast of Barstow. CR 1500 north 12.0 miles, FSR 1500 east 10.0 miles.

BELFAIR (B-2)

ALDRICH LAKE (Dept. of Natural Resources)
4 units, water, picnic area, lake, trail, boat launch, fishing, elev. 50'.
West of Belfair. Take State Highway 300 southwest 13 miles to Maggie Lake Road. Turn right, follow to Dewatto Road and turn left, go 2.1 miles to Robbins Lake Road, after .6 mile turn right, camp is .7 mile.

CAMP SPILLMAN (Dept. of Natural Resources)
6 units, water, picnic area, trail for hiker/horse/motorbike, fishing, elev. 60'.
Northwest of Belfair. Head southwest on State Highway 300 approximately 1 mile and turn right on Sandhill Road. At the Y take Goat Ranch Road to the left. The third road on the right leads to the campground.

GREEN MOUNTAIN HORSE CAMP (Dept. of Natural Resources)
9 units, water, trail, horse facilities, elev. 100'.
North of Belfair. Head southwest on State Highway 300

approximately 1 mile and turn right on Sandhill Road. Stay right at the Y an additional 8 miles to Green Mountain Road. This will lead to the campground.

HOWELL LAKE (Dept. of Natural Resources)
6 units, water, picnic area, trail for hiker/horse/motorbike, boat launch, fishing, elev. 50'.
West of Belfair. State Highway 300 southwest approximately 4 miles and turn right on Haven Lake Road. Stay left at Y and follow to Howell Lake.

R. F. KENNEDY (Dept. of Natural Resources)
8 units, picnic area, water, boat launch, dock, elev. 50'.
South of Belfair. State Highway 3 south 4.0 miles, State Highway 302 southeast 12.0 miles, Longbranch Road approximately 5 miles south. Campground is 2 miles northwest of Longbranch on Whiteman Cove.

TAHUYA RIVER HORSE CAMP (Dept. of Natural Resources)
9 units, water, fishing, trails for hiker/horse/motorbike, horse facilities, elev. 60'.
Northwest of Belfair. Head southwest on State Highway 300 approximately 1 mile and turn right on Sandhill Road. At the Y take Goat Ranch Road to the left. The second road on the left leads to the campground.

TOONERVILLE (Dept. of Natural Resources)
4 units, picnic area, trails for hiker/horse/motorbike, elev. 60'.
Northwest of Belfair. Head southwest on State Highway 300 approximately 1 mile and turn right on Sandhill Road. At the Y take Goat Ranch Road to the left. The first road on the right leads you to the campground, it's about 4 miles.

TWIN LAKES (Dept. of Natural Resources)
6 units, picnic area, boat launch, fishing, elev. 60'.
Northwest of Belfair. Head southwest on State Highway 300 approximately 1 mile and turn right on Sandhill Road. At the Y take Goat Ranch Road to the left, the fourth road on the right leads to the campground.

BOYDS (F-1)

DAVIS LAKE (Colville National Forest)
4 units, trailers to 18', boat launch, boating, fishing, elev. 4600'.
Northwest of Boyds. US Highway 395 north .5 mile, FSR 480 northwest 8.0 miles.

BURLINGTON (C-1)

BLANCHARD HILL, LILY & LIZARD LAKES (Dept. of Natural Resources)
9 campsites, trails for hiker/horse, horse facilities.
Northeast of Burlington. I-5 north to exit #240, Samish Lake Road .5 mile, Barrel Springs Road 1.0 mile, Road SW-C-100 1.5 miles to campground.

HUTCHINSON CREEK (Dept. of Natural Resources)
15 units, on Hutchinson Creek.
Northeast of Burlington. State Highway 20 east 6.5 miles, State Highway 9 north 16.0 miles, campground is 2.0 miles east of Acme, off Mosquito Lake Road, on Hutchinson Creek.

WALKER VALLEY ATV (Dept. of Natural Resources)
5 units, trails for hikers/horses/trailbikes/4-wheelers.
South of Burlington. State Highway 20 east 5.5 miles, State Highway 9 south 7.5 miles, campground is 2.5 miles east of Big Lake.

CARSON (C-5)

CREST (Gifford Pinchot National Forest)
3 units, trailers to 18', no water, trails to Pacific Crest Trail & Indian Heaven Wilderness, horse facilities, elev. 3500'.
Northwest of Carson. CR 92135 northwest 9.0 miles, FSR 6517 east 1.5 miles, FSR 65 northwest 8.0 miles, FSR 60 east 1.8 miles.

FALLS CREEK HORSE CAMP (Gifford Pinchot National Forest)
10 units, trailers to 18', fishing, horse trails, loading ramp, 2 corrals, trailhead to Indian Heaven Wilderness & historic Indian race track, elev. 3500'.
Northwest of Carson. CR 92135 northwest 9.0 miles, FSR 6517 (Warren Gap Road) east 1.5 miles, FSR 65 north 12.5 miles.

CASTLE ROCK (B-5)

WINSTON CREEK (Dept. of Natural Resources)
10 campsites, wheelchair access.
Northeast of Castle Rock. I-5 north 23.0 miles, US 12 east 21.0 miles to Mayfield Lake. Campground is 5 miles southeast of Mayfield Lake along Longbell County Road.

CHELAN (E-2)

BIG CREEK (Wenatchee National Forest)
3 tent units, boat-in only, shelter, stream, boating, swimming, fishing, water skiing, nearby waterfall, elev. 1100'.
Northwest of Chelan. Boat northwest 27.0 miles.

CORRAL CREEK (Wenatchee National Forest)
2 tent units, boat-in only, lake, boating, swimming, fishing, water skiing, elev. 1100'.
Northwest of Chelan. Boat northwest 27.6 miles.

DEER POINT (Wenatchee National Forest)
6 tent units, boat-in only, lake, boating, fishing, swimming, water skiing, elev. 1100'.
Northwest of Chelan. Boat northwest 21.7 miles.

DOMKE FALLS (Wenatchee National Forest)
4 tent units, lake, boating, fishing, swimming, water skiing, boat-in only, elev. 1100'.
Northwest of Chelan. Boat 37.5 miles northwest.

DOMKE LAKE (Wenatchee National Forest)
6 tent units, boat-in/hike-in/fly-in only, lake, boat rental, boating, swimming, fishing, elev. 2200'.
Northwest of Chelan. Boat northwest 40.0 miles, Trail #1280 south 3.0 miles.

GRAHAM HARBOR CREEK (Wenatchee National Forest)
13 tent units, boat-in only, shelter, stream, boating, fishing, swimming, water skiing, elev. 1100'.
Northwest of Chelan. Boat northwest 31.0 miles.

GROUSE MOUNTAIN SPRING (Wenatchee National Forest)
4 units, trailers to 18', piped water, adjacent to Devil's Backbone ORV trails, elev. 4500'.
Northwest of Chelan. US Highway 97 west 3.1 miles, CR 10 northwest 16.0 miles, FSR 5900 west 8.1 miles.

HANDY SPRING (Wenatchee National Forest)
1 tent unit, adjacent to Devil's Backbone ORV trails, elev. 6000'.
Northwest of Chelan. US Highway 97 west 3.1 miles, CR 10 northwest 16.0 miles, FSR 5900 west 14.5 miles, FSR 114 south .7 mile.

HATCHERY (Wenatchee National Forest)
2 tent units, boat-in/hike-in/fly-in only, stream, swimming, fishing, elev. 2200'.
Northwest of Chelan. Boat northwest 40.0 miles, Trail #1280 3.0 miles south, boat southeast 1.0 miles.

HOLDEN (Wenatchee National Forest)
2 tent units, boat-in only, stream, fishing, entry to Glacier Peak Wilderness, elev. 3200'.
Northwest of Chelan. Boat northwest 41.2 miles, FSR 8301 west 11.1 miles.

JUNIOR POINT (Wenatchee National Forest)
5 units, no water, adjacent to Devil's Backbone ORV trails, elev. 6600'.
Northwest of Chelan. US Highway 97 west 3.1 miles, CR 10 northwest 16.0 miles, FSR 5900 west 14.3 miles.

LUCERNE (Wenatchee National Forest)
2 tent units, boat-in only, well, lake, boating, fishing, swimming, water skiing, Domke Lake trailhead, elev. 1100'.
Northwest of Chelan. Boat northwest 41.2 miles.

MITCHELL CREEK (Wenatchee National Forest)
11 tent units, boat-in only, picnic area w/shelter, stream, boating, fishing, swimming, water skiing, elev. 1100'.
Northwest of Chelan. Boat northwest 14.9 miles.

MOORE POINT (Wenatchee National Forest)
6 tent units, boat-in only, lake, boating, swimming, fishing, water skiing, hiking, elev. 1100'.
North of Chelan. Boat northwest 43.0 miles.

PRINCE CREEK (Wenatchee National Forest)
5 tent units, boat-in only, picnic area, stream, boating, fishing, swimming, water skiing, hiking, elev. 1100'.
Northwest of Chelan. Boat northwest 35.2 miles.

RAMONA TRAILHEAD (Wenatchee National Forest)
7 tent units, trailers to 22', stream, fishing, water skiing, hiking, elev. 2000'.
Northwest of Chelan. US Highway 97 west 3.1 miles, CR 10 northwest 16.0 miles, FSR 5900 west 3.1 miles, FSR 8410 to campground.

REFRIGERATOR HARBOR (Wenatchee National Forest)
4 tent units, boat-in only, lake, Domke Lake trailhead, elev. 1100'.
Northwest of Chelan. Boat northwest 41.0 miles.

SAFETY HARBOR (Wenatchee National Forest)
4 tent units, boat-in only, stream, no tables, boating, fishing, swimming, water skiing, elev. 1100'.
Northwest of Chelan. Boat northwest 25.0 miles.

SOUTH NAVARRE (Wenatchee National Forest)
4 tent units, horse camping, stock water, summit trail, elev. 6000'.
Northwest of Chelan. State Highway 150 northwest 5.8 miles, CR 10 north 16 miles, FSR 8200 northwest .5 mile.

CHEWELAH (F-1)

CHEWELAH PARK (City)
Campsites, water, creek.
In Chewelah. Follow signs to city park.

CLE ELUM (D-3)

BEVERLY (Wenatchee National Forest)
16 units, trailers to 22', river, fishing, near horse & motorcycle trails, elev. 3200'.
North of Cle Elum. US Highway 97 east 8.0 miles, CR 107 north 13.0 miles, FSR 9737 north 4.0 miles.

BUCK MEADOWS (Wenatchee National Forest)
5 units, trailers to 18', pit toilets, horse & motorcycle trails, stream, fishing, elev. 4200'.
South of Cle Elum. I-90 southeast 12.0 miles, CR 9123 south 3.0 miles, CR 51 northwest 2.0 miles, FSR 33 northwest 6.0 miles, FSR 3300 south 8.0 miles, FSR 31 south 5.0 miles.

DE ROUX (Wenatchee National Forest)
4 tent units, stream, fishing, hiking trail, elev. 3800'.
North of Cle Elum. US Highway 97 east 8.0 miles, CR 107 north 13.0 miles, FSR 9737 northwest 8.0 miles.

FISH LAKE (Wenatchee National Forest)
15 tent units, stream, fishing, hiking, pit toilets, primitive, elev. 3400'.
Northwest of Cle Elum. State Highway 903 northwest 11.2 miles, CR 903 northwest 10.7 miles, FSR 4330 northeast 11.0 miles.

HANEY MEADOWS (Wenatchee National Forest)
18 units, group sites, horse loading & tethering facilities, hiking trails.
Northeast of Cle Elum. US Highway 97 east 12.0 miles, US Highway 97 north 8.1 mile, FSR 9722 east 10.0 mile.

ICEWATER CREEK (Wenatchee National Forest)
17 units, picnic area, water, trail, fishing, hiking.
South of Cle Elum. I-90 southeast 12.0 miles, CR 9123

south 3.0 miles, CR 51 northwest 2.0 miles, FSR 33 northwest 3.0 miles.

INDIAN CAMP (Dept. of Natural Resources)
9 tent units, river.
North of Cle Elum. I-90 to exit #85, State Highway 970 east 6.9 miles, Teanaway Road west .6 mile, West Fork Teanaway Road .6 mile south, Middle Fork Teanaway Road west 3.9 miles.

OWHI (Wenatchee National Forest)
23 walk-in units, picnic area, Cooper Lake - no motors, boat launch, boating, swimming, fishing, trailhead to Pacific Crest Trail & Alpine Lakes Wilderness, elev. 2800'.
Northwest of Cle Elum. State Highway 903 northwest 11.2 miles, CR 903 northwest 9.7 miles, FSR 46 northwest 4.9 miles, FSR 4616 north .2 mile.

QUARTZ MOUNTAIN (Wenatchee National Forest)
3 units, trailers to 18', piped water, horse and ORV trails, elev. 6100'.
South of Cle Elum. I-90 southeast 12.0 miles, CR 9123 south 3.0 miles, CR 51 northwest 2.0 miles, FSR 33 northwest 6.0 miles, FSR 3330 south 8.0 miles, FSR 1904 west 4.0 miles, FSR 3100 northwest 7.0 miles.

RED MOUNTAIN (Wenatchee National Forest)
12 tent units, river, pit toilets, hiking, fishing, elev. 2200'.
Northwest of Cle Elum. State Highway 903 northwest 11.2 miles, CR 903 northwest 8.3 miles.

RED TOP (Wenatchee National Forest)
3 units, no trailers - rough road, agate beds, pit toilet, fire lookout, horse trails, elev. 5100'.
Northeast of Cle Elum. US Highway 97 east 12.0 miles, US Highway 97 north 6.1 miles, FSR 9702 approximately 10 miles to campground. Near Red Top Lookout.

SCATTER CREEK (Wenatchee National Forest)
12 units, trailers to 32', river, fishing, elev. 3300'.
Northwest of Cle Elum. State Highway 903 northwest 11.2 miles, CR 903 northwest 10.7 miles, FSR 4330 northeast 10.9 miles.

SOUTH FORK MEADOW (Wenatchee National Forest)
4 units, trailers to 18', stream, fishing, hiking/motorcycle trails, elev. 3500'.
South of Cle Elum. I-90 southeast 12.0 miles, CR 9123 south 3.0 miles, CR 51 northwest 2.0 miles, FSR 33 northwest 11.0 miles.

TAMARACK SPRING (Wenatchee National Forest)
2 tent units, pit toilet, horse & cycle trails, elev. 4700'.
South of Cle Elum. I-90 southeast 12.0 miles, CR 9123 south 3.0 miles, CR 51 northwest 2.0 miles, FSR 33 northwest 6.0 mile, FSR 3330 south 8.0 miles, FSR 3120 east 2.0 miles.

TEANAWAY (Dept. of Natural Resources)
6 campsites.
East of Cle Elum. Campground is 8.0 miles northwest of junction of Teanaway River Road and US Highway 97.

TUCQUALA MEADOWS (Wenatchee National Forest)
9 units, trailers to 18', stream, trailhead to Alpine Lakes Wilderness, elev. 3400'.
Northwest of Cle Elum. State Highway 903 northwest 11.2 miles, CR 903 northwest 10.7 miles, FSR 4330 northeast 12.9 miles.

COLVILLE (F-1)

DOUGLAS FALLS (Dept. of Natural Resources)
19 campsites, drinking water, wheelchair access, waterfalls, hiking trails.
East of Colville. State Highway 20 east .5 mile, Aladdin Road & Douglas Falls County Road 5.0 miles north to campground.

FLODELLE CREEK (Dept. of Natural Resources)
8 campsites, drinking water.
East of Colville. State Highway 20 east 21.0 miles, Flodelle Creek Road .2 mile to campground.

LITTLE TWIN LAKES (Colville National Forest)
20 units, trailers to 18', well, lake, boat launch, boating, fishing, rough road, elev. 3800'.

East of Colville. State Highway 20 east 12.5 miles, CR 4939 northeast 4.2 miles, FSR 9413 north .9 mile.

ROCKY LAKE (Dept. of Natural Resources)
8 campsites, drinking water, boat launch.
Southeast of Colville. Campground is located 3.0 miles southeast of Colville, off State Highway 395, on Rocky Lake.

WILLIAMS LAKE (Dept. of Natural Resources)
10 campsites, drinking water, lake.
North of Colville. Campground is 16.0 miles north of Colville along Echo County Road, on Williams Lake.

CONCONULLY (D-1)

KERR (Okanogan National Forest)
11 units, trailers to 22', stream, fishing, elev. 3100'.
Northwest of Conconully. CR 2361 northwest 1.8 miles, FSR 38 northwest 2.0 miles.

SUGARLOAF (Okanogan National Forest)
5 units, trailers to 22', lake - speed limit, boat launch, boating, swimming, fishing, elev. 2400'.
Northeast of Conconully. CR 4015 northeast 4.5 miles.

TIFFANY SPRINGS (Okanogan National Forest)
6 tent units, stream, elev. 6800'.
Northwest of Conconully. CR 2017 southwest 1.8 miles, FSR 364 northwest 21.2 miles, FSR 370 northeast 7.0 miles.

CONCRETE (C-1)

BOULDER CREEK (Mt. Baker-Snoqualmie National Forest)
10 units, trailers to 18', elev. 1100'.
North of Concrete. North off State Highway 20 at milepost #82, north 9.6 miles to FSR 11, north 5.4 miles to campground. Located 1 mile west of Baker Lake.

CASCADE ISLANDS (Dept. of Natural Resources)
19 campsites, drinking water, river.
East of Concrete. State Highway 20 east 19.0 miles, located on Cascade River.

GRANDY LAKE (Skagit County)
20 campsites, pit toilets, primitive, fishing, hiking.
Northeast of Concrete. State Highway 20 east to Baker Lake Road, turn left and proceed about 4-5 miles where you will find signs leading to Grandy Lake Park.

MAPLE GROVE (Mt. Baker-Snoqualmie National Forest)
6 tent units, boat-in or hike-in only, lake, boating, swimming, fishing, water skiing, trails, elev. 700'.
North of Concrete. North off State Highway 20 at milepost #82, north 9.6 miles to FSR 11, north 2.4 miles, FSR 1106 east 2.0 miles, cross dam to FSR 1107 to trailhead, hike 3.0 miles north along east shore of Baker Lake.

PARK CREEK (Mt. Baker-Snoqualmie National Forest)
12 units, trailers to 18', stream, elev. 800'.
North of Concrete. North off State Highway 20 at milepost #82, north 9.6 miles to FSR 11, north 7.4 miles, FSR 1144 northwest .1 mile. Campground is 1 mile from Baker Lake.

SHANNON CREEK (Mt. Baker-Snoqualmie National Forest)
20 units, trailers to 22', on Baker Lake, picnic area, boating, swimming, fishing, water skiing, elev. 800'.
North of Concrete. North off State Highway 20 at milepost #82, north 9.6 miles to FSR 11, north 12.2 miles, FSR 3830 southeast .5 mile.

SAUK PARK (Skagit County)
20 campsites, primitive, no toilets, picnic area, fishing, hiking.
Southeast of Concrete. State Highway 20 east to Rockport, cross Lower Government Bridge and turn right on Sauk Valley Road. Park is .3 mile.

COOK (D-6)

BUCK CREEK RIDGE (Dept. of Natural Resources)
6 campsites, trails for hikers & horses.
Northeast of Cook. State Highway 14 east to White Salmon, campground is 3.0 miles north of White Salmon on west side of White Salmon River.

COUGAR (B-5)

LAKE MERRILL (Dept. of Natural Resources)
7 campsites, picnic area, drinking water, boat launch.
North of Cougar. Located on the east shore of Lake Merrill, 6.0 miles north of Cougar.

LOWER LEWIS RIVER FALLS (Gifford Pinchot National Forest)
20 units, trailers to 20', no drinking water, on Upper Lewis River, fishing, hiking, trails, waterfalls, elev. 1300'.
East of Cougar. FSR 90 northeast 30.0 miles.

COUPEVILLE (B-1)

RHODODENDRON (Dept. of Natural Resources)
8 campsites, drinking water, hiking trails.
Southeast of Coupeville. State Highway 525 southeast 2.0 miles.

CURLEW (E-1)

DEER CREEK SUMMIT (Colville National Forest)
4 units, trailers to 18', hiking trails, elev. 4600'.
East of Curlew. CR 602 east 11.5 miles.

DARRINGTON (C-1)

BUCK CREEK (Mt. Baker-Snoqualmie National Forest)
49 units, trailers to 22', shelter, picnic area, fishing, hiking, elev. 1200'.
East of Darrington. State Highway 530 north 7.7 miles, FSR 26 east 15.2 miles.

CLEAR CREEK (Mt. Baker-Snoqualmie National Forest)
7 units, trailers to 22', picnic area, river, fishing, Frog Lake Trailhead, elev. 600'.
Southeast of Darrington. Mountain Loop Highway southeast 4.0 miles.

SULPHUR CREEK (Mt. Baker-Snoqualmie National Forest)
16 units, trailers to 18', fishing, Sulphur Creek Trailhead, elev. 1500'.
East of Darrington. State Highway 530 north 7.7 miles, FSR 26 east 22.5 miles.

WHITECHUCK (Mt. Baker-Snoqualmie National Forest)
5 units, trailers okay, river, boating, fishing, hiking, elev. 900'.
Southeast of Darrington. Mountain Loop Highway southeast 10.2 miles.

WILLIAM C. DEARINGER (Dept. of Natural Resources)
16 campsites, wheelchair access.
Northeast of Darrington. Sauk Prairie Road northeast 2.0 miles, East Sauk Prairie Road 4.0 miles to campground.

DAYTON (F-5)

EDMISTON (Umatilla National Forest)
9 units, some trailers, picnic area, elev. 5300'.
Southeast of Dayton. US Highway 12 to Kendall-Skyline Road N910, campground is 21 miles southeast of Dayton.

GODMAN (Umatilla National Forest)
8 tent units, picnic area, no water, trails, horse facilities, elev. 6050'.
Southeast of Dayton. CR 118 southeast 14.8 miles, FSR 46 south 11.0 miles.

STOCKADE SPRING (Umatilla National Forest)
2 tent units, no trailers, piped water, picnic area, elev. 4600'.
Southeast of Dayton. US Highway 12 to Kendall-Skyline Road N910, campground is 18 miles southeast of Dayton.

TEEPEE (Umatilla National Forest)
7 units, trailers to 18', elev. 5700'.
Southeast of Dayton. CR 118 southeast 14.8 miles, FSR 46 south 11.0 miles, FSR 4608 northeast 5.0 miles.

ELBE (C-4)

ALDER LAKE (Dept. of Natural Resources)
25 campsites, drinking water, picnic area, group shelter, boat launch, fishing.
West of Elbe. State Highway 7 south to Pleasant Valley Road, follow road 3.5 miles keeping left at the Y.

ELBE HILLS ORV TRAILHEAD (Dept. of Natural Resources)
5 campsites, no water, picnic area, group shelter, jeep trails.
East of Elbe. State Highway 706 east 6.1 miles, turn left just before National and follow 3.7 miles to campground.

ELDON (B-2)

LENA CREEK (Olympic National Forest)
12 units, trailers to 22', well, swimming, fishing, Lena Lakes Trailhead, elev. 700'.
Northwest of Eldon. US Highway 101 north 1.7 miles, FSR 25 west 9.0 miles.

LENA LAKE (Olympic National Forest)
10 tent units, hike-in only, no tables, fishing, swimming, geology, mountain climbing, elev. 1800'.
Northwest of Eldon. US Highway 101 north 1.7 miles, FSR 25 west 9.0 miles, Trail #810 for 4.0 miles to campground.

ELLENSBURG (D-4)

ESMERELDA (Wenatchee National Forest)
3 units, trailers to 18', stream, fishing, horse trails, elev. 4200'.
North of Ellensburg. US Highway 97 east 8.0 miles, CR 107 north 13.0 miles, FSR 9737 northwest 9.0 miles.

LION ROCK SPRING (Wenatchee National Forest)
3 tent units, picnic area, pit toilets, hiking trails, horse & motorcycle trails nearby, elev. 6300'.
North of Ellensburg. CR 179 north 12.4 miles, FSR 35 north 9.7 miles, FSR 124 west .8 mile.

ENTIAT (D-3)

SPRUCE GROVE (Wenatchee National Forest)
2 tent units, no trailers, river, fishing, elev. 2900'.
Northwest of Entiat. US Highway 97 southwest 1.4 miles, CR 371 northwest 25.2 miles, FSR 5100 northwest 9.8 miles.

BIG HILL (Wenatchee National Forest)
1 tent unit, shelter, no water, dispersed camping, elev. 6800'.
Northwest of Entiat. US Highway 97 southwest 1.4 miles, CR 371 northwest 25.2 miles, FSR 317 northwest 3.5 miles, FSR 298 north 7.9 miles, FSR 298A north 1.5 miles.

HALFWAY SPRING (Wenatchee National Forest)
5 tent units, no trailers, piped water, hiking, dispersed camping, elev. 5000'.
Northwest of Entiat. US Highway 97 southwest 1.4 miles, CR 371 northwest 25.2 miles, FSR 317 northwest 3.5 miles, FSR 298 north 2.0 miles.

SHADY PASS (Wenatchee National Forest)
1 tent unit, no trailers, picnic table, dispersed camping, toilet, elev. 5400'.
Northwest of Entiat. US Highway 97 southwest 1.4 miles, CR 371 northwest 25.2 miles, FSR 317 northwest 3.5 miles, FSR 298 north 5.1 miles.

THREE CREEK (Wenatchee National Forest)
3 tent units, river, fishing, nearby hiking trail, elev. 2900'.
Northwest of Entiat. US Highway 97 southwest 1.4 miles, CR 371 northwest 25.2 miles, FSR 5100 northwest 10.5 miles.

ENUMCLAW (B-3)

CORRAL PASS (Mt. Baker-Snoqualmie National Forest)
20 tent units, stream, near Mountain Goat Reserve & Norse Peak Wilderness, berry picking, primitive, horse ramp, elev. 5600'.
Southeast of Enumclaw. State Highway 410 southeast 31.0 miles, FSR 7174 east 6.1 miles.

ECHO LAKE (Mt. Baker-Snoqualmie National Forest)
13 units, hike-in only, shelter, swimming, fishing, elev. 3800'.
Southeast of Enumclaw. State Highway 410 southeast 32.1 miles, FSR 185 east 6.7 miles, Trail #1176 northeast 5.2 miles.

EVANS CREEK (Mt. Baker-Snoqualmie National Forest)
26 units, shelter, stream, trailbike & ATV trails, elev. 3200'.
South of Enumclaw. State Highway 165 south of Buckley 12.0 miles, continue 7.0 miles onto gravel road, FSR 7920 about 2 miles to campground.

FORKS (A-2)

BEAR CREEK (Dept. of Natural Resources)
10 campsites, drinking water, hiking.
Northeast of Forks. US Highway 101 northeast 15 miles to milepost #206; campground is 2.0 miles east of Sappho on Hoh River Road.

COTTONWOOD (Dept. of Natural Resources)
7 campsites, drinking water, river, boat launch.
Southeast of Forks. US Highway 101 south 13 miles, Oil City Road 4.0 miles, Road H-4060 .9 mile to campground.

HOH OXBOW (Dept. of Natural Resources)
6 campsites, picnic area, river, boat launch.
Southeast of Forks. US Highway 101 south 14 miles, located on north side of Hoh bridge, at milepost #176.

HUELSDONK (Dept. of Natural Resources)
5 campsites, on Hoh River.

Southeast of Forks. US Highway 101 south 14 miles, Hoh-Clearwater Mainline Road east 10 miles.

KLAHANIE (Olympic National Forest)
15 primitive campsites, trailers to 22', rain forest, river, fishing, elev. 300'.
East of Forks. US Highway 101 north 1.7 miles, FSR 29 east 5.4 miles.

MINNIE PETERSON (Dept. of Natural Resources)
6 campsites, river, drinking water.
Southeast of Forks. US Highway 101 south 12 miles, Upper Hoh Road east 4.5 miles.

SOUTH FORK HOH (Dept. of Natural Resources)
3 campsites, river.
Southeast of Forks. US Highway 101 south 14 miles, Hoh-Clearwater Mainline Road east 6.6 miles, Road H-1000 north 7.4 miles.

SPRUCE CREEK (Dept. of Natural Resources)
5 campsites.
Southeast of Forks. US Highway 101 south 13 miles, Valley Road 7.0 miles to campground.

WILLOUGHBY CREEK (Dept. of Natural Resources)
3 campsites, river.
Southeast of Forks. Take US Highway 101 south 2 miles, Upper Hoh Road east 3.5 miles.

YAHOO LAKE (Dept. of Natural Resources)
6 walk-in campsites, trails.
Southeast of Forks. US Highway 101 south 14 miles, Hoh-Clearwater Mainline Road east 12.5 miles, Road C-3000 north 4.8 miles, Road C-3100 east 5.5 miles, keep left .6 mile to trailhead.

FORT SPOKANE (F-2)

CRYSTAL COVE (Coulee Dam Rec. Area)
Tent units, hike-in or boat-in only, on Spokane River Arm of Lake Roosevelt.

North of Fort Spokane. Located on Spokane River Arm of Lake Roosevelt.

PONDEROSA (Coulee Dam Rec. Area)
Tent units, hike-in or boat-in only, on Spokane River Arm of Lake Roosevelt.
North of Fort Spokane. Located on Spokane River Arm of Lake Roosevelt.

GOLDENDALE (D-5)

ROOSEVELT PARK (Corps of Engineers)
10 units, trailers okay, boat launch, fishing, windsurfing, picnic area.
Southeast of Goldendale. US Highway 97 south 11 miles, State Highway 14 east 32 miles to campground.

GRAND COULEE (F-2)

PLUM POINT (Coulee Dam Rec. Area)
Tent units, boat dock, hike-in or boat-in only, on Lower Lake Roosevelt.
Southwest of Grand Coulee. Located on Lower Lake Roosevelt.

GRANITE FALLS (C-1)

BEAVER PLANT LAKE (Dept. of Natural Resources)
6 campsites, hike-in only.
Southeast of Granite Falls. CR FH7 east 15 miles, FSR 3015 4.0 miles staying left at T to parking lot, trail 1.1 miles to campground.

BEDAL (Mt. Baker-Snoqualmie National Forest)
18 units, trailers to 22', picnic area, river, fishing, elev. 1300'.
East of Granite Falls. CR FH7 east 30.1 miles, FSR 20 northeast 6.5 miles.

BOARDMAN CREEK (Mt. Baker-Snoqualmie National Forest)
8 tent units, 2 trailer sites, group sites, fishing, elev. 1200'.
East of Granite Falls. CR FH7 16.6 miles east.

BOARDMAN LAKE (Mt. Baker-Snoqualmie National Forest)
8 tent units, hike-in only, lake-no motors, swimming, fishing, trails, elev. 3100'.
Southeast of Granite Falls. CR FH7 east 15.5 miles, FSR 4020 south 6.9 miles, Trail #704 south 1.0 miles.

LOWER ASHLAND LAKE (Dept. of Natural Resources)
6 campsites, hike-in only.
Southeast of Granite Falls. CR FH7 east 15 miles, FSR 3015 for 4.0 miles staying left at T to parking lot, trail 2.0 miles to campground.

MT. PILCHUCK REC. AREA (Mt. Baker-Snoqualmie National Forest)
12 units, trailers to 32', group sites, picnic area, water, hiking, elev. 3000'.
East of Granite Falls. CR FH7 east 12 miles, FSR 42 southwest 6.9 miles to campground.

RED BRIDGE (Mt. Baker-Snoqualmie National Forest)
16 units, trailers to 32', river, fishing, elev. 1300'.
East of Granite Falls. CR FH7 east 18.1 miles.

TWIN FALLS LAKE (Dept. of Natural Resources)
5 campsites, hike-in only.
Southeast of Granite Falls. CR FH7 east 15 miles, FSR 3015 for 4.0 miles staying left at T to parking lot, trail 3.5 miles to campground.

UPPER ASHLAND LAKE (Dept. of Natural Resources)
6 campsites, hike-in only.
Southeast of Granite Falls. CR FH7 east 15 miles, FSR 3015 for 4.0 miles staying left at T to parking lot, trail 1.5 miles to campground.

HOODSPORT (B-3)

LILLIWAUP (Dept. of Natural Resources)
6 campsites, creek, drinking water.
Northwest of Hoodsport. Take Cushman-Jorstad Road 4.0 miles northeast of Lake Cushman to Lilliwaup Creek and campground.

MELBOURNE (Dept. of Natural Resources)
5 units, lake.
Northwest of Hoodsport. US Highway 101 north, Jorsted Creek Road northwest 5.5 miles, west 2.5 miles keeping left at Y.

HUMPTULIPS (A-3)

CAMPBELL TREE GROVE (Olympic National Forest)
14 units, trailers to 16', pit toilets, pump, stream, fishing, hiking, primitive, elev. 1100'.
Northeast of Humptulips. US Highway 101 northeast 4.0 miles, FSR 2204 northeast 21.5 miles to campground.

HUNTERS (F-1)

CLOVER LEAF (Coulee Dam Rec. Area)
6 tent units, boat dock, water, picnic area, swimming beach.
North of Hunters. Located just south of Gifford on State Highway 25.

DETILLON (Coulee Dam Rec. Area)
12 campsites, boat-in only, water, boat dock.
South of Hunters. State Highway 20 south to its junction with Spokane River, boat east about 9 miles upriver to campground.

ENTERPRISE (Coulee Dam Rec. Area)
13 campsites, boat-in only.
Southwest of Hunters. Located on east bank of FDR Lake approximately 8 miles southwest of Hunters.

JONES BAY (Coulee Dam Rec. Area)
6 campsites, boat-in only, dock, elev. 1282'.
Southwest of Hunters. Located approximately 6 miles east of San Poil River's junction with FDR Lake, on lake's shore.

ILWACO (A-5)

WESTERN LAKES (Dept. of Natural Resources)
3 units, fishing, trails.
Northeast of Ilwaco. US Highway 101 northeast 16 miles, State Highway 4 east 4.3 miles, C-line uphill .9 mile north, Road C-4000 east 1.4 miles, Road C-2600 north .9 mile, campground road .3 mile.

INDEX (C-2)

BIG GREIDER LAKE (Dept. of Natural Resources)
5 campsites, hike-in only, trails.
Northwest of Index. US Highway 2 west to Sultan, Sultan Basin Road northeast to Greider Creek and Reflection Ponds, hike-in 3.0 miles to Big Greider Lake.

BOULDER LAKE (Dept. of Natural Resources)
9 campsites, hike-in only, trails.
Northwest of Index. US Highway 2 west to Sultan, Sultan Basin Road northeast 20 miles to Elk Creek, hike 3.2 miles to Boulder Lake and campsites.

CUTTHROAT LAKE (Dept. of Natural Resources)
10 campsites, hike-in only, trails.
Northwest of Index. US Highway 2 west to Sultan, Sultan Basin Road northeast 22 miles to Gilbert Creek Trailhead #37, hike-in 3.0 miles to lake and campsites.

LITTLE GREIDER LAKE (Dept. of Natural Resources)
9 campsites, hike-in only, trails.
Northwest of Index. US Highway 2 west to Sultan, Sultan Basin Road northeast to Greider Creek and Reflection Ponds, hike-in 5.5 miles to Little Greider Lake.

SAN JUAN (Mt. Baker-Snoqualmie National Forest)
10 tent units, river, fishing, primitive, elev. 1500'.
Northeast of Index. CR 63 northeast 14 miles.

TROUBLESOME CREEK (Mt. Baker-Snoqualmie National Forest)
30 units, trailers to 22', group area, picnic area, river, fishing, interpretive trail, hiking, on site caretaker, elev. 1300'.
Northeast of Index. CR 63 northeast 12 miles.

IONE (G-1)

EDGEWATER (Colville National Forest)
23 units, trailers to 20', piped water, river, boat launch, boating, fishing, water skiing, elev. 2100'.
Northwest of Ione. State Highway 31 south 1 mile, CR 9345 east .3 mile, CR 3669 north 2.0 miles, FSR 33101 for 1.8 miles to campground.

KETTLE FALLS (F-1)

BRADBURY BEACH (Coulee Dam Rec. Area)
5 units, trailers okay, boat ramp, picnic area, water, elev. 1285'.
South of Kettle Falls. State Highway 25 south 8 miles to campground.

CANYON CREEK (Colville National Forest)
12 units, trailers to 32', well, fishing, primitive, elev. 2200'.
West of Kettle Falls. State Highway 20 northwest 14.5 miles, FSR 136 south .2 mile.

HAAG COVE (Coulee Dam Rec. Area)
8 units, trailers okay, water, picnic area, boat dock.
Southwest of Kettle Falls. Take State Highway 20 across the river and follow the west bank of FDR Lake south to the campground.

KAMLOOPS ISLAND (Coulee Dam Rec. Area)
17 campsites, trailers okay, boat dock, water.

Northwest of Kettle Falls. Take State Highway 20 across the river and follow US Highway 395 north 4 miles to campground.

KETTLE RIVER (Coulee Dam Rec. Area)
12 units, trailers okay, water, boat dock, elev. 1237'.
Northwest of Kettle Falls. Take State Highway 20 across the river and follow US Highway 395 up the Kettle River to the camp, just below Boyd.

NE LAKE ELLEN (Colville National Forest)
11 units, trailers to 22', well, boat launch, boating, swimming, fishing, elev. 2400'.
Southwest of Kettle Falls. US Highway 395 northwest 3.5 miles, State Highway 20 south 4.0 miles, CR 2014 southwest 4.5 miles, FSR 2014 southwest 5.5 miles.

NORTH GORGE (Coulee Dam Rec. Area)
12 units, trailers okay, water, boat ramp, dock, on Columbia River, elev. 1282'.
North of Kettle Falls. State Highway 25 northeast 18 miles.

SHEEP CREEK (Dept. of Natural Resources)
20 campsites, picnic area, drinking water.
Northeast of Kettle Falls. State Highway 25 northeast 33 miles to Northport, campground is 4.0 miles northwest on Sheep Creek.

SHERMAN PASS (Colville National Forest)
9 units, trailers okay, picnic area, piped water, hiking, horse trails, elev. 5300'.
West of Kettle Falls. State Highway 20 west 22 miles to Sherman Pass.

SNAG COVE (Coulee Dam Rec. Area)
6 units, trailers okay, water, on west bank of Columbia River, boat dock.
Northwest of Kettle Falls. State Highway 20 across the river and follow US Highway 395 north 4 miles, take road to right for 8 miles to campground.

SUMMER ISLAND (Coulee Dam Rec. Area)
Tent units, boat dock, hike-in or boat-in only,

Southwest of Kettle Falls. Located on Upper Lake Roosevelt.

TROUT LAKE (Colville National Forest)
4 units, trailers to 18', piped water, boat launch, boating, fishing, elev. 3000'.
West of Kettle Falls. US 395 northwest 3.5 miles, State 20 west 5.5 miles, FSR 20 northwest 5.0 miles.

LEAVENWORTH (D-3)

ALPINE MEADOW (Wenatchee National Forest)
4 tent units, river, fishing, elev. 2700'.
Northwest of Leavenworth. US Highway 2 northwest 15.9 miles, State Highway 207 north 4.0 miles, Chiwawa Loop Road east 1.0 mile, FSR 6200 northwest 19.5 miles.

ATKINSON FLAT (Wenatchee National Forest)
8 units, trailers to 22', river, fishing, elev. 2500'.
Northwest of Leavenworth. US Highway 2 northwest 15.9 miles, State Highway 207 north 4.0 miles, Chiwawa Loop Road east 1.0 mile, FSR 6200 northwest 15.0 miles.

DEER CAMP (Wenatchee National Forest)
3 tent units, stream, elev. 4000'.
Northeast of Leavenworth. US Highway 2 east .3 mile, State Highway 209 north 14.5 miles, Chiwawa Loop Road northeast 3.0 miles, FSR 6100 north 1.5 miles, FSR 6101 northeast 2.0 miles.

DEEP CREEK (Wenatchee National Forest)
3 camping units, stream, fishing, elev. 2000'.
North of Leavenworth. US Highway 2 east .3 mile, State Highway 209 north 14.5 miles, Chiwawa Loop Road northeast 3.0 miles, FSR 6100 north 2.2 miles.

FINNER (Wenatchee National Forest)
3 tent units, trailers to 32', piped water, stream, fishing, trails, elev. 2500'.
Northwest of Leavenworth. US Highway 2 northwest 15.9 miles, State Highway 207 north 4.0 miles, Chiwawa Loop Road east 1.0 miles, FSR 6200 northwest 11.0 miles.

GRASSHOPPER MEADOWS (Wenatchee National Forest)
5 tent units, river, fishing, elev. 2000'.
Northwest of Leavenworth. US Highway 2 northwest 15.9 miles, State Highway 207 north 8.4 miles, Chiwawa Loop Road northwest .9 mile, FSR 6400 northwest 7.9 miles.

LAKE CREEK (Wenatchee National Forest)
8 tent units, stream, fishing, elev. 2300'.
Northwest of Leavenworth. US Highway 2 northwest 15.9 miles, State Highway 207 north 9.0 miles, FSR 6500 west 9.8 miles.

LITTLE WENATCHEE FORD (Wenatchee National Forest)
3 tent units, stream, fishing, hiking trails, primitive, elev. 2900'.
Northwest of Leavenworth. US Highway 2 northwest 15.9 miles, State Highway 207 north 9.0 miles, FSR 6500 northwest 14.7 miles.

MEADOW CREEK (Wenatchee National Forest)
4 units, fishing, elev. 2300'.
North of Leavenworth. US Highway 2 northwest 15.9 miles, State Highway 207 northeast 4.0 miles, Chiwawa Loop Road east 1.0 mile, FSR 6200 2.4 miles northeast.

NAPEEQUA (Wenatchee National Forest)
5 units, some trailers to 32', river, fishing, Glacier Peak Wilderness entrance, elev. 2000'.
Northwest of Leavenworth. US Highway 2 northwest 15.9 miles, State Highway 207 north 8.4 miles, Chiwawa Loop Road northwest .9 mile, FSR 6400 northwest 5.9 miles.

NINETEEN MILE (Wenatchee National Forest)
4 units, trailers to 22', river, fishing, elev. 2600'.
Northwest of Leavenworth. US Highway 2 northwest 15.9 miles, State Highway 207 north 4.0 miles, Chiwawa Loop Road east 1.0 mile, FSR 6200 northwest 18.0 miles.

PHELPS CREEK (Wenatchee National Forest)
7 tent units, fishing, horse trails to Glacier Peak Wilderness, horse ramp, elev. 2800'.
Northwest of Leavenworth. US Highway 2 northwest 15.9 miles, State Highway 207 north 4.0 miles, Chiwawa Loop Road east 1.0 miles, FSR 6200 northwest 21.0 miles.

ROCK CREEK (Wenatchee National Forest)
4 units, fishing, trails, elev. 2500'.
Northwest of Leavenworth. US Highway 2 northwest 15.9 miles, State Highway 207 north 4.0 miles, Chiwawa Loop Road east 1.0 mile, FSR 6200 northwest 15.0 miles.

SCHAEFER CREEK (Wenatchee National Forest)
6 units, fishing, river, elev. 2600'.
Northwest of Leavenworth. US Highway 2 northwest 15.9 miles, State Highway 207 north 4.0 miles, Chiwawa Loop Road east 1.0 mile, FSR 6200 north 15.8 miles.

SODA SPRINGS (Wenatchee National Forest)
5 tent units, stream, fishing, trails, elev. 2000'.
Northwest of Leavenworth. US Highway 2 northwest 15.9 miles, State Highway 207 north 9.0 miles, FSR 6500 west 7.2 miles.

THESEUS CREEK (Wenatchee National Forest)
2 units, trailers to 18', fishing, primitive, elev. 2300'.
Northwest of Leavenworth. US Highway 2 northwest 15.9 miles, State Highway 207 northwest 9.0 miles, FSR 6500 west 6.0 miles, FSR 6701 west 4.5 miles.

WHITE RIVER FALLS (Wenatchee National Forest)
5 tent units, river, fishing, Glacier Peak Wilderness entrance, elev. 2100'.
Northwest of Leavenworth. US Highway 2 northwest 15.9 miles, State Highway 207 north 8.4 miles, Chiwawa Loop Road northwest .9 mile, FSR 6400 northwest 9.0 miles.

WHITEPINE (Wenatchee National Forest)
4 units, trailers to 22', stream, fishing, elev. 1900'.
Northwest of Leavenworth. US Highway 2 northwest 24.9 miles, FSR 6950 west .5 mile.

LOOMIS (D-1)

CHOPAKA LAKE (Dept. of Natural Resources)
15 units, drinking water, lake, boat launch, fishing.
Northwest of Loomis. Palmer lake Road north 2.1 miles, Toats Coulee Road west 1.4 miles, Chopaka Creek Road northwest 5.1 miles, right 2.0 miles to campground.

COLD SPRINGS (Dept. of Natural Resources)
9 campsites in mountainous area, spring water, picnic area, stream, trails for hiker/horse, horse facilities.
Northwest of Loomis. Palmer Lake Road north 2.1 miles. Toats Coulee Road west 5.6 miles, OM-T-1000 2.1 miles, Cold Creek Road .4 mile, keep right 1.8 miles, veer left 2.7 miles to campground.

LONG SWAMP (Okanogan National Forest)
2 units, trailers to 18', stream, hiking, elev. 5500'.
West of Loomis. Palmer Lake Road north 2.1 miles, Toats Coulee Road north 1.0 mile, FSR 39 west 20.5 miles.

NORTH FORK NINE MILE (Dept. of Natural Resources)
11 units, drinking water, picnic area, stream, fishing.
Northwest of Loomis. Palmer Lake Road north 2.1 miles, Toats Coulee Road west 5.6 miles, OM-T-1000 2.5 miles.

PALMER LAKE (Dept. of Natural Resources)
6 units, lake.
North of Loomis. Palmer Lake Road north 8.5 miles.

TOATS COULEE (Dept. of Natural Resources)
9 units, picnic area, stream.
Northwest of Loomis. Palmer Lake Road north 2.1 miles, Toats Coulee Road west 5.5 miles.

MARBLEMOUNT (C-1)

CASCADE ISLAND (Dept. of Natural Resources)
10 tent/trailer sites, primitive.
Southeast of Marblemount. Follow Cascade River Road to South Cascade Road and campground.

MARBLE CREEK (Mt. Baker-Snoqualmie National Forest)
24 units, picnic area, pit toilets, fishing, elev. 900'.
East of Marblemount. Cascade River Road to FSR 15, campground is 8.0 miles east.

MINERAL PARK (Mt. Baker-Snoqualmie National Forest)
5 tent units, picnic area, pit toilets, river, fishing, elev. 1400'.
East of Marblemount. Cascade River Road to FSR 15, campground is 16.0 miles.

MONTESANO (A-4)

CHETWOOT (Olympic National Forest)
8 tent units, hike-in or boat-in only, lake, pit toilets, boating, swimming, fishing, water skiing, hiking trails, elev. 800'.
North of Montesano. CR 58 north 12.0 miles, FSR 22 north 21.0 miles, FSR 23 north 2.5 miles, Trail #878 east .5 mile.

TENAS (Olympic National Forest)
9 tent units, hike-in or boat-in only, lake, no picnic tables, boating, swimming, fishing, hiking trails, elev. 800'.
North of Montesano. CR 58 north 12.0 miles, FSR 22 north 20.0 miles, FSR 2202 north 2.0 miles, Trail #878 .5 mile west.

WYNOOCHEE FALLS (Olympic National Forest)
18 tent units, river, fishing, elev. 1000'.
North of Montesano. CR 141 north 18.5 miles, FSR 22 north 26.7 miles, FSR 2312 northeast 10.0 miles.

NACHES (D-4)

BUMPING CROSSING (Wenatchee National Forest)
12 units, trailers to 18', river, fishing, hiking, reduced service, elev. 3200'.
Northwest of Naches. US Highway 12 west 4.3 miles, State Highway 410 northwest 28.6 miles, FSR 1800 northwest 9.9 miles.

BUMPING DAM (Wenatchee National Forest)
28 units, trailers to 18', river, fishing, reduced service, elev. 3400'.
Northwest of Naches. US Highway 12 west 4.3 miles, State Highway 410 northwest 27.8 miles, FSR 174 southwest 10.8 miles, FSR 1602 north .6 mile.

CLEAR LAKE SOUTH (Wenatchee National Forest)
26 units, picnic area, stream, lake - 5 mph speed limit, boating, fishing, hiking, reduced service, elev. 3100'.
Southwest of Naches. US Highway 12 west 35.6 miles, FSR 143 south .9 mile, FSR 1312 south 1.0 mile.

CROW CREEK (Wenatchee National Forest)
15 units, trailers to 18', fishing, ORV, reduced service, elev. 2900'.
Northwest of Naches. US Highway 12 west 4.3 miles, State Highway 410 northwest 24.8 miles, FSR 1900 northwest 3.1 miles.

DEEP CREEK (Wenatchee National Forest)
6 units, trailers to 18', trailhead into Cougar Lakes Area, elev. 4300'.
West of Naches. US Highway 12 west 4.3 miles, State Highway 410 northwest 27.8 miles, FSR 174 southwest 13.3 miles, FSR 162 southwest 7.0 miles.

GRANITE LAKE (Wenatchee National Forest)
8 units, trailers to 18', boating, swimming, fishing, elev. 5000'.
West of Naches. US Highway 12 west 4.3 miles, State Highway 410 northwest 27.8 miles, FSR 174 southwest 13.9 miles, FSR 163 southwest 3.7 miles.

HALFWAY FLAT (Wenatchee National Forest)
12 units, trailers to 18', river, fishing, reduced service, elev. 2500'.
Northwest of Naches. US Highway 12 west 4.3 miles, State Highway 410 northwest 21.2 miles, FSR 1704 northwest 2.9 miles.

HUCKLEBERRY (Wenatchee National Forest)
8 tent units, river, fishing, berry picking, elev. 5300'.
Northwest of Naches. US Highway 12 west 4.3 miles, State Highway 410 northwest 24.3 miles, FSR 197 northwest 3.0 miles, FSR 182 for 7.0 miles to campground.

LONGMIRE MEADOW (Wenatchee National Forest)
13 units, trailers to 18', river, fishing, elev. 2800'.
Northwest of Naches. US Highway 12 west 4.3 miles, State Highway 410 northwest 24.3 miles, FSR 197 northwest 4.1 miles.

LOST LAKE (Wenatchee National Forest)
3 tent units, boating, swimming, fishing, elev. 3500'.
West of Naches. US Highway 12 west 22.6 miles, FSR 143 south .2 mile, FSR 1402 southeast 4.6 miles.

MILK POND (Wenatchee National Forest)
5 units, lake, fishing, hiking.
West of Naches. US Highway 12 west 4.3 miles, State Highway 410 northwest 25.0 miles, FSR 1708 northeast 1.7 miles.

PENINSULA (Wenatchee National Forest)
19 units, trailers to 18', lake, boating, swimming, fishing, boat landing, water skiing, reduced service, elev. 3000'.
Southwest of Naches. US Highway 12 west 22.6 miles, FSR 143 south 2.9 miles, FSR 1200 west 1.0 mile.

PINE NEEDLE (Wenatchee National Forest)
6 tent units, river, fishing, reduced service, elev. 3000'.
Northwest of Naches. US Highway 12 west 4.3 miles, State Highway 410 northwest 30.8 miles.

PLEASANT VALLEY (Wenatchee National Forest)
14 units, trailers to 22', picnic area, river, fishing, hiking, elev. 3300'.
Northwest of Naches. US Highway 12 west 4.3 miles, State Highway 410 northwest 37.0 miles.

RIMROCK PUBLIC BOAT LANDING (Wenatchee National Forest)
5 units, lake, fishing, swimming, boating, water skiing.
West of Naches. US Highway 12 west 29.6 miles to campground.

SODA SPRINGS (Mt. Baker-Snoqualmie National Forest)
19 units, trailers to 18', picnic area, well, natural mineral spring, fishing, mountain climbing, reduced service, elev. 3100'.
Northwest of Naches. US Highway 12 west 4.3 miles, State Highway 410 northwest 27.8 miles, FSR 174 southwest 5.0 miles.

SOUTH FORK (Wenatchee National Forest)
9 units, trailers to 18', river, fishing, reduced service, elev. 3000'.
Southwest of Naches. US Highway 12 west 22.6 miles, FSR 143 south 4.1 miles, FSR 1326 south .5 mile.

WILD ROSE (Wenatchee National Forest)
8 units, trailers to 32', no water, river, fishing, reduced service, elev. 2400'.
West of Naches. US Highway 12 west 20.4 miles to campground.

NEAH BAY (A-1)

ERICKSON'S BAY (Olympic National Park)
15 tent units, hiking, beach access, elev. 80'.
South of Neah Bay. Located at Ozette Lake, take road from Seiku.

NORTH BEND (C-3)

COMMONWEALTH (Mt. Baker-Snoqualmie National Forest)
6 units, no trailers, picnic area, stream, near Pacific Crest National Scenic Trail, hiking, horse trails, mountain climbing, elev. 3000'.
Southeast of North Bend. I-90 southeast 22.0 miles, FSR 58 north .2 mile. Located at Snoqualmie Pass.

MINE CREEK (Dept. of Natural Resources)
17 campsites, river, wheelchair access.
East of North Bend. Campground is located 8.0 miles east of town, on Middle Fork Snoqualmie River.

OKANOGAN (E-1)

LEADER LAKE (Dept. of Natural Resources)
16 units, picnic area, boat launch, fishing.
West of Okanogan. State Highway 20 west 8.4 miles, Leader Lake Road .4 mile to campground.

ROCK CREEK (Dept. of Natural Resources)
6 units, drinking water, picnic area.
Northwest of Okanogan. State Highway 20 west 9.8 miles, Loup Loup Creek Road north 3.9 miles to campground.

ROCK LAKES (Dept. of Natural Resources)
8 units, hiking trails, fishing.
Northwest of Okanogan. State Highway 20 west 9.8 miles, Loup Loup Creek Road north 4.8 miles, Rock Lakes Road northwest 5.8 miles to campground.

OLYMPIA (B-3)

FALL CREEK (Dept. of Natural Resources)
8 campsites, drinking water, creek, wheelchair access, horse & hiking trails, horse facilities.
Southwest of Olympia. Campground is located 5.0 miles west of Delphi entrance to Capitol Forest Multiple Use Area, on Fall Creek.

HOLLYWOOD (Dept. of Natural Resources)
10 campsites, drinking water, trails for horses/hikers/trailbikes.
Southwest of Olympia. Campground is 6.0 miles northwest of Littlerock on Waddell Creek, in Capitol Forest Multiple Use Area.

MARGARET MCKENNY (Dept. of Natural Resources)
18 campsites, drinking water, trails for horses/hikers/trailbikes, horse facilities.
Southwest of Olympia. Campground is 3.0 miles northwest of Littlerock along Waddell Creek Road, in Capitol Forest Multiple Use Area.

MIMA FALLS TRAILHEAD (Dept. of Natural Resources)
3 campsites, trails for hikers & horses, horse facilities.
Southwest of Olympia. Campground is 4.0 miles west of Littlerock at trailhead, in Capitol Forest Multiple Use Area.

MT. MOLLY (Dept. of Natural Resources)
10 campsites, drinking water, trails for horses/hikers/trailbikes.
Southwest of Olympia. Campground is 6.0 miles northwest of Littlerock on Waddell Creek, in Capitol Forest Multiple Use Area.

NORTH CREEK (Dept. of Natural Resources)
5 campsites, drinking water, trails for hikers & horses.

Southwest of Olympia. Campground is 6.0 miles northeast of Oakville on Cedar Creek Road, in Capitol Forest Multiple Use Area.

PORTER CREEK (Dept. of Natural Resources)
16 campsites, drinking water, trails for hikers/horses/trailbikes, horse facilities.
Southwest of Olympia. Campground is 5.0 miles northeast of Porter, on Porter Creek Road, in Capitol Forest Multiple Use Area.

SHERMAN VALLEY "Y" (Dept. of Natural Resources)
11 campsites, drinking water, trails for hikers & horses.
Southwest of Olympia. Campground is 9.0 miles west of Littlerock along Cedar Creek, in Capitol Forest Multiple Use Area.

ORIENT (F-1)

PIERRE LAKE (Colville National Forest)
15 units, trailers to 32', well, boat launch, boating, swimming, fishing, water skiing, elev. 2000'.
Northeast of Orient. CR 1510 east 3.8 miles, CR 1500 north 3.2 miles.

SUMMIT LAKE (Colville National Forest)
5 units, no trailers, well, boat launch, boating, fishing, elev. 3600'.
Northeast of Orient. CR 1510 east 3.8 miles, CR 1500 north 5.0 miles.

PACKWOOD (C-4)

BYPASS (Gifford Pinchot National Forest)
5 tent units, hike-in only, wilderness area, creek, elev. 5500'.
Southeast of Packwood. US Highway 12 southwest 2.0 miles, FSR 21 south 11.0 miles, FSR 2150 northwest 3.0 miles to Chambers Lake Campground, Trail #96 about 4 miles to campground.

DOG LAKE (Wenatchee National Forest)
11 units, trailers to 18', boat launch, fishing, hiking trails, reduced service, elev. 4300'.
Northeast of Packwood. US Highway 12 northeast 22.2 miles.

LOST LAKE (Gifford Pinchot National Forest)
2 wilderness camp areas, 8 tent units, hike-in only, lake, elev. 5200'.
Southeast of Packwood. Leave US Highway 12 in Packwood on Packwood Lake Road and follow 4 miles to end, Trail #78 to Packwood Lake then additional 3.6 miles to Lost Lake.

SODA SPRINGS (Gifford Pinchot National Forest)
8 tent units, fishing, trailhead to William O. Douglas Wilderness, elev. 3200'.
Northeast of Packwood. US Highway 12 northeast 8.9 miles, FSR 45 west 1.0 miles, FSR 4510 northwest 5.0 miles.

SUMMIT CREEK (Gifford Pinchot National Forest)
7 units, fishing, rough road, elev. 2400'.
Northeast of Packwood. US Highway 12 northeast 8.9 miles, FSR 45 west 1.0 miles, FSR 4510 northwest 2.1 miles.

WALUPT LAKE HORSE CAMP (Gifford Pinchot National Forest)
6 units, trailers to 18', stream, horse trails/tethering area, trailhead to Goat Rocks Wilderness, elev. 3900'.
Southeast of Packwood. US Highway 12 southwest 2.7 miles, FSR 21 southeast 16.4 miles, FSR 2160 east 3.5 miles.

WHITE PASS LAKE (Wenatchee National Forest)
16 units, trailers to 18', lake - no motors, boat launch, Pacific Crest Trailhead, boating, swimming, fly fishing, hiking, reduced service, elev. 4500'.
Northeast of Packwood. US Highway 12 northeast 20.9 miles, FSR 1310 north .3 mile.

WHITE PASS HORSE CAMP (Wenatchee National Forest)
6 units, shelter, horse watering area & hitch rails, river, boating, swimming, fishing, hiking trails, elev. 3400'.
Northeast of Packwood. US Highway 12 northeast 20.9 miles, FSR 1310 north .3 mile to campground.

POMEROY (F-4)

ALDER THICKET (Umatilla National Forest)
6 units, no water, elev. 5100'.
South of Pomeroy. State Highway 128 south 9.1 miles, CR 107 south 7.7 miles, FSR 40 south 3.3 miles.

BIG SPRINGS (Umatilla National Forest)
15 units, picnic facilities, no water, elev. 5000'.
Southeast of Pomeroy. State Highway 128 southeast 9.1 miles, CR 107 south 7.7 miles, FSR 40 south 8.8 miles to Clearwater Lookout, FSR 42 about 3 miles to campground road.

FOREST BOUNDARY (Umatilla National Forest)
5 units, trailers to 32', elev. 4400'.
South of Pomeroy. State Highway 128 south 9.1 miles, CR 107 south 7.7 miles, FSR 40 south .1 mile.

LADY BUG (Umatilla National Forest)
Camping area, pit toilet, no drinking water, near Wenaha-Tucannon Wilderness, swimming, fishing.
South of Pomeroy. CR 101 southwest 17.6 miles, FSR 47 southwest 12.1 miles, FSR 4713 southwest 1.2 miles to campground.

MISERY SPRINGS (Umatilla National Forest)
5 tent units, no water, hiking, elev. 6000'.
Southeast of Pomeroy. State Highway 128 south 9.1 miles, CR 107 south 7.7 miles, FSR 40 southeast 16.2 miles, FSR 4030 south .5 mile.

PANJAB (Umatilla National Forest)
2 units, trailers to 18', no water, river, trails, fishing in Tucannon River, elev. 3000'.
Southwest of Pomeroy. CR 101 southwest 17.6 miles, FSR 47 southwest 12.1 miles, FSR 4713 south .2 mile.

PANJAB TRAILHEAD (Umatilla National Forest)
7 tent units, fishing, hiking, horse trails, elev. 3400'.
Southwest of Pomeroy. CR 101 southwest 17.6 miles, FSR 47 southwest 12.1 miles, FSR 4713 south 2.3 miles.

SPRUCE SPRING (Umatilla National Forest)
3 units, trailers to 18', no water, elev. 5100'.
South of Pomeroy. State Highway 128 south 9.1 miles, CR 107 south 7.7 miles, FSR 40 southeast 10.9 miles.

TEAL (Umatilla National Forest)
10 units, picnic facilities, no water, hiking, elev. 5600'.
South of Pomeroy. State Highway 128 south 9.1 miles, CR 107 south 7.7 miles, FSR 40 south 8.8 miles, FSR 200 south .3 miles, located just past Clearwater Lookout Tower.

TUCANNON (Umatilla National Forest)
13 units, trailers to 18', group picnic area, no water, river, fishing, elev. 2600'.
Southwest of Pomeroy. CR 101 southwest 17.6 miles, FSR 47 southwest 8.1 miles, FSR 160 south .2 mile.

WICKIUP (Umatilla National Forest)
5 units, primitive facilities, no drinking water, elev. 5800'.
South of Pomeroy. State Highway 128 south 9.1 miles, CR 107 south 7.7 miles, FSR 40 south 17.0 miles, FSR 44 for 3.0 miles to campground.

PORT ANGELES (A-1)

DEER PARK (Olympic National Park)
18 tent units, water, elev. 5400'.
Southeast of Port Angeles. US Highway 101 east 6.0 miles, Blue Mountain Road south 18.0 miles to end of road and campground.

LYRE RIVER (Dept. of Natural Resources)
10 campsites, drinking water.
West of Port Angeles. US Highway 101 west 5.0 miles, State Highway 112 west 17.0 miles to Lyre River and campground.

QUEETS (A-2)

COPPERMINE BOTTOM (Dept. of Natural Resources)
10 campsites, boat launch, hiking.
Northeast of Queets. US Highway 101 southeast 5.4 miles, Clearwater Road north 12.6 miles, Road C-1010 for 1.5 miles to campground.

UPPER CLEARWATER (Dept. of Natural Resources)
9 campsites, drinking water, boat launch.
Northeast of Queets. US Highway 101 southeast 5.4 miles, Clearwater Road north 12.9 miles, Road C-3000 for 3.2 miles to campground.

QUILCENE (B-2)

DOSEWALLIPS (Olympic National Park)
32 units, restrooms, handicap access, summer nature program, elev. 1540'.
Southwest of Quilcene. US Highway 101 south 13.0 miles, D River Road west 15.0 miles.

RANDLE (C-4)

CAT CREEK (Gifford Pinchot National Forest)
6 units, trailers to 16', on Cispus River, fishing, elev. 3000'.
Southeast of Randle. Take County Road south 3.1 miles, FSR 23 southeast 15.7 miles, FSR 21 east 6.1 miles.

CHAIN-OF-LAKES (Gifford Pinchot National Forest)
3 units, trailers to 16', lake - speed limits, swimming, fishing, hiking trails, near Mt. Adams Wilderness, trailhead to horse camp, elev. 4400'.
Southeast of Randle. Take County Road south 3.1 miles, FSR 23 southeast 28.9 miles, FSR 2329 north 1.2 miles, FSR 22 north 1.0 mile.

COUNCIL LAKE (Gifford Pinchot National Forest)
11 units, trailers to 16', lake - speed limit, boating, swimming, fishing, hiking trails, near Mt. Adams Wilderness, elev. 4300'.

Southeast of Randle. Take County Road south 3.1 miles, FSR 23 southeast 30.2 miles, FSR 2334 west 1.2 miles.

HORSESHOE LAKE (Gifford Pinchot National Forest)
10 units, trailers to 16', lake - speed limit, primitive boat launch, boating, swimming, fishing, hiking trails, near Mt. Adams Wilderness, elev. 4200'.
Southeast of Randle. Take County Road south 3.1 miles, FSR 23 southeast 28.9 miles, FSR 2329 northeast 6.8 miles, FSR 78 west 1.3 miles.

KEENES HORSE CAMP (Gifford Pinchot National Forest)
14 units, trailers to 22', stream, horse trails/ramp/corrals/water trough, hiking trails, near Mt. Adams Wilderness, elev. 4300'.
Southeast of Randle. Take County Road southeast 3.1 miles, FSR 23 southeast 28.9 miles, FSR 2329 southeast 7.2 miles, FSR 82 west .1 mile.

KILLEN CREEK (Gifford Pinchot National Forest)
8 units, trailers to 22', trailhead for climbing north face of Mt. Adams, berry picking, elev. 4400'.
Southeast of Randle. Take County Road south 3.1 miles, FSR 23 southeast 28.9 miles, FSR 2329 southeast 6.2 miles, FSR 72 west .1 mile.

OLALLIE LAKE (Gifford Pinchot National Forest)
5 units, trailers to 22', lake - speed limit, boating, swimming, fishing, elev. 2700'.
Southeast of Randle. Take County Road south 3.1 miles, FSR 23 southeast 28.9 miles, FSR 2329 north .8 mile, FSR 5601 north .6 mile.

POLE PATCH (Gifford Pinchot National Forest)
12 units, stream, berry picking, rough road, elev. 4400'.
South of Randle. Take County Road south 2.0 miles, FSR 25 south 20.3 miles, FSR 28 east 2.8 miles, FSR 77 north 6.1 miles.

SPRING CREEK (Gifford Pinchot National Forest)
3 units, trailers to 16', hiking, near Mt. Adams Wilderness, berry picking, elev. 4300'.

Southeast of Randle. Take County Road south 3.1 miles, FSR 23 southeast 28.9 miles, FSR 2329 northeast 7.5 miles, FSR 85 west 1.3 miles.

REPUBLIC (E-1)

KETTLE RANGE (Colville National Forest)
9 units, trailers to 22', picnic area, well, hiking trails, elev. 5400'.
East of Republic. State Highway 21 east .5 mile, State Highway 20 east 18.0 miles.

RIVERSIDE (E-1)

CRAWFISH LAKE (Okanogan National Forest)
18 units, trailers to 32', boat launch, boating, fishing, elev. 4500'.
East of Riverside. CR 9320 east 17.7 miles, FSR 3612 south 1.7 miles, FSR 3525 southeast .4 mile.

SAN JUAN ISLANDS (B-1)

BLIND ISLAND STATE PARK (Washington State Parks)
4 tent sites, boat-in only, buoys, primitive, no drinking water, beach access.
In San Juan Islands. Blind Island is located north of Shaw Island.

CLARK ISLAND STATE PARK (Washington State Parks)
8 tent sites, boat-in only, buoys, primitive, no drinking water, beachcombing, scuba diving area, fishing, must pack-out garbage.
In San Juan Islands. Clark Island is located northeast of Orcas Island.

CYPRESS HEAD (Dept. of Natural Resources)
5 units, boat-in only, picnic area, mooring buoys.
In San Juan Islands. On Cypress Island.

CYPRESS ISLAND/PELICAN BEACH (Dept. of Natural Resources)
6 campsites, boat-in only, buoys, hiking trails.
In San Juan Islands. On Cypress Island, 4.0 miles north of Cypress Head, on northeast side.

DOE ISLAND STATE PARK (Washington State Parks)
5 tent sites, boat-in only, floats, primitive, no drinking water, scuba diving area, small secluded island.
In San Juan Islands. Doe Island is located southeast of Orcas Island.

HOPE ISLAND STATE PARK (Washington State Parks)
5 tent sites, boat-in only, primitive, no drinking water.
In San Juan Islands. Hope Island is located in Skagit Bay, 2.0 miles north of entrance to Swinomish Bay, near Whidbey Island.

JAMES ISLAND (Washington State Parks)
13 campsites, boat-in only, buoys, no drinking water, picnic facilities, hiking trails, scuba diving.
In San Juan Islands. Located on James Island.

JONES ISLAND (Washington State Parks)
21 campsites, boat-in only, buoys, scuba diving, picnic facilities, hiking.
In San Juan Islands. Located on Jones Island.

LUMMI ISLAND (Dept. of Natural Resources)
4 campsites, boat-in only.
In San Juan Islands. Located on southeast tip of Lummi Island, 1.0 miles south of Reil Harbor.

MATIA ISLAND STATE PARK (Washington State Parks)
6 tent sites, boat-in only, primitive, no drinking water, buoys & floats, scuba diving area, fishing.
In San Juan Islands. Located northeast of Orcas Island about 2.5 miles.

ORCAS ISLAND/OBSTRUCTION PASS (Dept. of Natural Resources)
9 campsites, boat-in or hike-in only, buoys, hiking trails.
In San Juan Islands. Campground is located 5.0 miles southwest of Rosario, on Orcas Island.

ORCAS ISLAND/POINT DOUGHTY (Dept. of Natural Resources)
4 campsites, boat-in only, buoys.
In San Juan Islands. Campground is on north end of Orcas Island; 3.0 miles northwest of Eastsound.

PATOS ISLAND STATE PARK (Washington State Parks)
4 tent sites, boat-in only, primitive, no drinking water, buoys, good fishing, hiking.
In San Juan Islands. Patos Island is located 4.0 miles northwest of Sucia Island.

POSEY ISLAND STATE PARK (Washington State Parks)
1 tent site, primitive, no drinking water, boat-in only - small boats with shallow draft.
In San Juan Islands. Posey Island is very accessible to San Juan Island, north of Roche Harbor.

SADDLEBAG ISLAND STATE PARK (Washington State Parks)
5 tent sites, boat-in only, primitive, no drinking water, fishing, beachcombing, crabbing.
In San Juan Islands. Saddlebag Island is located north of Anacortes and east of Guemes Island.

SKAGIT ISLAND (Washington State Parks)
Boat camping, no facilities on shore, mooring buoys, boat-in only.
In San Juan Islands. Skagit Island is located in Skagit Bay.

STRAWBERRY/LOON ISLAND (Dept. of Natural Resources)
6 campsites, boat-in only.
In San Juan Islands. Loon Island is located .5 mile west of Cypress Island.

SEQUIM (A-2)

DUNGENESS FORKS (Olympic National Forest)
9 tent units, well, river, pit toilet, fishing, hiking trails, elev. 1000'.

Southwest of Sequim. US Highway 101 southwest 4.0 miles, CR 9537 south 4.5 miles, FSR 2880 southwest 3.0 miles.

EAST CROSSING (Olympic National Forest)
9 units, trailers to 16', well, river, fishing, hiking, primitive, elev. 1200'.
South of Sequim. US Highway 101 southeast 3.0 miles, Dungeness River Road south 11.0 miles.

SPOKANE (G-2)

DRAGOON CREEK (Dept. of Natural Resources)
25 campsites, drinking water, wheelchair access.
North of Spokane. US Highway 395 north 9.0 miles to Dragoon Creek and campground.

LONG LAKE (Dept. of Natural Resources)
16 campsites, drinking water, lake, boat launch, Indian paintings.
Northwest of Spokane. State Highway 291 to Long Lake, campground is 3.0 miles east of Long Lake Dam over Lapray Bridge Road #1108.

TAMPICO (D-5)

AHTANUM (Dept. of Natural Resources)
11 campsites, drinking water, trail, creek, fishing.
West of Tampico. Head northwest out of Tampico along A-2000 Middle Fork Ahtanum Creek Road for 9.5 miles. Campground is on left.

CLOVER FLATS (Dept. of Natural Resources)
9 campsites, drinking water, rough roads.
West of Tampico. Head northwest out of Tampico along A-2000 Middle Fork Ahtanum Creek Road approximately 18.7 miles to campground.

SNOW CABIN (Dept. of Natural Resources)
8 campsites, creek, fishing, horse facilities.
West of Tampico. Head northwest out of Tampico along A-2000 Middle Fork Ahtanum Creek Road 14.0 miles, keep left at Y, campground is 2.6 miles further.

TREE PHONES (Dept. of Natural Resources)
14 campsites, picnic area, group shelter, trail, horse facilities, creek.
West of Tampico. Head northwest out of Tampico along A-2000 Middle Fork Ahtanum Creek Road for approximately 15.2 miles. Turn left and proceed .1 mile to campground.

TONASKET (E-1)

LYMAN LAKE (Okanogan National Forest)
4 units, trailers to 32', lake, fishing, elev. 2900'.
Southeast of Tonasket. State Highway 20 east 12.6 miles, CR 9455 southeast 13.0 miles, FSR 3785 south 2.4 miles, FSR 358 northwest .2 mile.

TROUT LAKE (D-5)

BIRD CREEK (Dept. of Natural Resources)
7 campsites, picnic area.
Northeast of Trout Lake. Take road east to Glenwood, campground is 6.0 miles northwest of Glenwood along the Bird Creek County Road, on Bird Creek.

COLD SPRINGS (Gifford Pinchot National Forest)
3 tent units, Mt. Adams Trailhead, primitive, elev. 5700'.
North of Trout Lake. State Highway 141 southeast .2 mile, CR 17 north 1.9 miles, FSR 80 north 3.5 miles, FSR 8040 north 8.0 miles.

FORLORN LAKES (Gifford Pinchot National Forest)
8 units, trailers to 18', no drinking water, lake - no motors, boating, swimming, fishing, primitive, elev. 3600'.
West of Trout Lake. State Highway 141 west 5.5 miles, FSR 24 west 2.5 miles, FSR 60 west 5.0 miles, FSR 6040 north 2.5 miles. This location offers a cluster of five small lakes.

GOOSE LAKE (Gifford Pinchot National Forest)
25 units, trailers to 18', no drinking water, lake - speed limit, boat launch, boating, swimming, fishing, primitive, elev. 3200'.

Southwest of Trout Lake. State Highway 141 southwest 5.5 miles, FSR 24 west 2.5 miles, FSR 60 southwest 5.2 miles.

ICE CAVE (Gifford Pinchot National Forest)
7 units, trailers to 18', picnic facilities, no water, lava tube cave, primitive, elev. 2800'.
Southwest of Trout Lake. State Highway 141 southwest 5.5 miles, FSR 24 west .9 mile, FSR 31 south .2 mile.

ISLAND CAMP (Dept. of Natural Resources)
6 campsites, winter sports.
Northeast of Trout Lake. Take road east to Glenwood, campground is 8.0 miles northwest of Glenwood along the Bird Creek County Road, on Bird Creek.

LEWIS RIVER (Gifford Pinchot National Forest)
4 tent units, on Upper Lewis River, swimming, fishing, hiking, primitive, elev. 1500'.
Northwest of Trout Lake. State Highway 141 west 1.4 miles, FSR 88 northwest 12.3 miles, FSR 8851 north 7.2 miles, FSR 100 west, 5.1 miles, FSR 3241 to campground.

LITTLE GOOSE (Gifford Pinchot National Forest)
28 units, trailers to 18', piped water, berry picking, stream, hiking trails, primitive, elev. 4000'.
Northwest of Trout Lake. State Highway 141 southwest 5.5 miles, FSR 24 northwest 10.1 miles.

MORRISON CREEK (Gifford Pinchot National Forest)
12 units, no water, Mt. Adams Wilderness Trailhead, elev. 4600'.
North of Trout Lake. State Highway 141 southeast .2 mile, CR 17 north 1.9 miles, FSR 80 north 3.5 miles, FSR 8040 north 6.1 miles.

MORRISON CREEK HORSE CAMP (Gifford Pinchot National Forest)
3 units, trailers to 18', horse corral & loading ramp, Mt. Adams Trailhead, elev. 4600'.
North of Trout Lake. State Highway 141 southeast .2 mile, CR 17 north 1.9 miles, FSR 80 north 3.5 miles, FSR 8040 north 6.0 miles.

SADDLE (Gifford Pinchot National Forest)
12 units, huckleberry area, primitive, no water, elev. 4200'.
Northwest of Trout Lake. State 141 southwest 5.5 miles, FSR 24 northwest 18.3 miles, FSR 2480 north 1.3 miles.

SMOKEY CREEK (Gifford Pinchot National Forest)
3 units, trailers to 22', berry picking, no water, elev. 3700'.
West of Trout Lake. State Highway 141 southwest 5.5 miles, FSR 24 northwest 7.3 miles.

SOUTH (Gifford Pinchot National Forest)
8 units, trailers to 18', well, huckleberry area, elev. 4000'.
Northwest of Trout Lake. State Highway 141 southwest 5.5 miles, FSR 24 northwest 18.3 miles, FSR 2480 east .3 mile.

TILLICUM (Gifford Pinchot National Forest)
49 units, trailers to 18', piped water, stream, hiking, berry picking, elev. 4300'.
Northwest of Trout Lake. State Highway 141 southwest 5.5 miles, FSR 24 northwest 19.1 miles.

TWIN FALLS (Gifford Pinchot National Forest)
4 units, on east bank of Upper Lewis River, fishing, primitive, elev. 2700'.
Northwest of Trout Lake. State Highway 141 west 1.4 miles, FSR 88 northwest 16.3 miles, FSR 150 north 5.2 miles.

WICKY SHELTER (Gifford Pinchot National Forest)
1 unit, log shelter for groups, hiking, primitive, elev. 4000'.
North of Trout Lake. State Highway 141 southeast .2 mile, CR 17 north 1.9 miles, FSR 80 for 3.5 miles, FSR 8040 north 1.5 miles.

TWISP (E-1)

FOGGY DEW (Okanogan National Forest)
13 units, trailers to 18', stream, hiking trails, elev. 2400'.
Southwest of Twisp. State Highway 20 east 2.0 miles, State Highway 153 south 12.2 miles, CR 1034 southwest 1.1 miles, FSR 4340 west 4.1 miles.

MYSTERY (Okanogan National Forest)
4 units, river, fishing, hiking trails, elev. 2800'.
West of Twisp. CR 9114 west 10.8 miles, FSR 44
northwest 7.3 miles.

ROADS END (Okanogan National Forest)
4 units, no trailers, river, fishing, hiking trails, elev. 3600'.
West of Twisp. CR 9114 west 10.8 miles, FSR 44
northwest 14.4 miles.

SOUTH CREEK (Okanogan National Forest)
4 units, trailers to 15', fishing, hiking trails, elev. 3100'.
West of Twisp. CR 9114 west 10.8 miles, FSR 44
northwest 11.3 miles.

USK (G-1)

PANHANDLE (Colville National Forest)
11 units, trailers to 22', piped water, river, boat launch,
boating, fishing, water skiing, elev. 2000'.
North of Usk. CR 91 east .3 mile, CR 7 north 16.2 miles.

SKOOKUM CREEK (Dept. of Natural Resources)
14 campsites, drinking water.
East of Usk. Campground is 4.0 miles east of Usk on
Skookum Creek.

VANCOUVER (B-6)

COLD CREEK (Dept. of Natural Resources)
7 campsites, picnic area w/shelter, drinking water, hiking
trails, horse facilities.
Northeast of Vancouver. Campground is 11.0 miles
southeast of Yacolt on Cedar Creek.

DOUGLAS CREEK (Dept. of Natural Resources)
7 campsites, picnic area, drinking water, hiking trails.
East of Vancouver. State Highway 14 east 16.0 miles to
Washougal. Campground is located 19.0 miles northeast
of Washougal River Valley, in Yacolt Multiple Use Area.

ROCK CREEK CAMP (Dept. of Natural Resources)
9 campsites, drinking water, trails for hikers & horses, horse facilities.
Northeast of Vancouver. Campground is located 9.0 miles southeast of Yacolt along Dole Valley County Road, on Rock Creek.

WOODLAND/BRATTON CANYON (Dept. of Natural Resources)
10 campsites, picnic area w/shelter, wheelchair access, drinking water.
Northeast of Vancouver. I-5 north 20.0 miles to Woodland, campground is 3.0 miles east of Woodland on CR 38.

WILBUR (F-2)

PENIX CANYON (BLM)
Campsites, boat ramp, boat-in or hike-in only.
North of Wilbur. Located on Lower Lake Roosevelt.

HALVERSON (BLM)
Campsites, boat-in or hike-in only.
North of Wilbur. Located on Lower Lake Roosevelt.

WILKESON (C-3)

EVANS CREEK O.R.V. CAMP (Mt. Baker-Snoqualmie National Forest)
26 units, trailers to 32', picnic area, elev. 3600'.
Northeast of Wilkeson. State Highway 165 southeast 3.5 miles.

WINTHROP (D-1)

BALLARD (Okanogan National Forest)
7 units, trailers to 22', river, fishing, elev. 2600'.
Northwest of Winthrop. State Highway 20 northwest 13.2 miles, CR 1163 northwest 6.9 miles, FSR 5400 northwest 2.1 miles.

CAMP FOUR (Okanogan National Forest)
5 units, trailers to 18', stream, fishing, elev. 2400'.
Northeast of Winthrop. CR 1213 north 6.6 miles, FSR 5160 northeast 11.3 miles.

CHEWUCH (Okanogan National Forest)
4 units, trailers to 16', stream, fishing, elev. 2200'.
Northeast of Winthrop. CR 1213 north 6.6 miles, FSR 5160 northeast 8.6 miles.

HARTS PASS (Okanogan National Forest)
5 tent units, no trailers, entrance to Pacific Crest National Scenic Trail & Pasayten Wilderness nearby, elev. 6200'.
Northwest of Winthrop. State Highway 20 northwest 13.2 miles, CR 1163 northwest 6.9 miles, FSR 5400 northwest 12.5 miles.

HONEYMOON (Okanogan National Forest)
5 units, stream, fishing, elev. 3300'.
Northwest of Winthrop. CR 1213 north 6.6 miles, FSR 5160 north 2.8 miles, FSR 5130 northwest 8.9 miles.

MEADOWS (Okanogan National Forest)
14 units, stream, access to Pacific Crest National Scenic Trail & Alpine Meadows, elev. 6200'.
Northwest of Winthrop. State Highway 20 northwest 13.2 miles, CR 1163 northwest 6.9 miles, FSR 5400 northwest 12.5 miles, FSR 5400-500 south 1.0 miles.

NICE (Okanogan National Forest)
4 units, stream, fishing, elev. 2700'.
North of Winthrop. CR 1213 north 6.6 miles, FSR 5160 north 2.8 miles, FSR 5130 northwest 3.8 miles.

RUFFED GROUSE (Okanogan National Forest)
4 units, stream, fishing, elev. 3200'.
Northwest of Winthrop. CR 1213 north 6.6 miles, FSR 5160 north 2.8 miles, FSR 5130 northwest 7.8 miles.

CAMPGROUND INDEX

ABBOTT CREEK - 21
AHTANUM - 120
ALDER FLAT - 29
ALDER GLEN - 15
ALDER LAKE - 92
ALDER SPRINGS - 47
ALDER THICKET - 113
ALDRICH LAKE - 79
ALLEN CREEK - 48
ALPINE MEADOW - 102
ALPINE SPRING - 68
APPLE CREEK - 63
ATKINSON FLAT - 102
BADGER LAKE - 73
BALLARD - 125
BARLOW CREEK - 35
BARLOW CROSSING - 35
BARNHOUSE - 48
BASSER DIGGINS - 15
BEAR CANYON - 68
BEAR CREEK - 59
BEAR CREEK - 94
BEAR PAW - 35
BEAR WALLOW CREEK - 70
BEAVER DAM - 74
BEAVER PLANT LAKE - 96
BEDAL - 96
BEECH CREEK - 33
BENNETT PARK - 49
BEVERLY - 85
BIG BEN - 20
BIG BEND - 41
BIG CREEK - 60
BIG CREEK - 70
BIG CREEK - 82
BIG GREIDER LAKE - 99
BIG HILL - 93
BIG LAKE WEST - 61
BIG RIVER - 16
BIG SPRING - 54
BIG SPRINGS - 113
BIG TWIN LAKES - 34
BILLY FIELDS - 49
BIRD CREEK - 121
BLACK PINE SPRINGS - 61
BLAIR LAKE - 49
BLANCHARD HILL, LILY & LIZARD LAKES - 81
BLIND ISLAND STATE PARK - 117
BOARDMAN CREEK - 97
BOARDMAN LAKE - 97
BOLAN LAKE - 22
BONNEY CROSSING - 73
BONNEY MEADOWS - 73
BOULDER CREEK & ANNEX - 66
BOULDER CREEK - 88
BOULDER FLAT - 34

127

BOULDER FLAT - 63
BOULDER LAKE - 73
BOULDER LAKE - 99
BOUNDARY - 72
BOX CANYON HORSE CAMP - 19
BRADBURY BEACH - 100
BRADLEY LAKE BOAT RAMP - 15
BREITENBUSH LAKE - 29
BUCK CREEK - 90
BUCK CREEK RIDGE - 90
BUCK MEADOWS - 85
BUCKHORN - 28
BULL BEND - 43
BUMPING CROSSING - 106
BUMPING DAM - 106
BUNCH GRASS MEADOWS - 67
BUNKER HILL - 63
BUTLER BAR - 55
BYPASS - 111
CABIN LAKE - 33
CALAMUT LAKE - 63
CAMP COMFORT - 67
CAMP FOUR - 126
CAMP SPILLMAN - 79
CAMP TEN - 29
CAMP WINDY - 73
CAMPBELL LAKE - 52
CAMPBELL TREE GROVE - 98
CAMPERS FLAT - 50
CANAL CREEK - 72
CANDLE CREEK - 21
CANYON CREEK - 100
CANYON MEADOWS - 39
CASCADE ISLAND - 105
CASCADE ISLANDS - 89
CASTLE ROCK - 37
CAT CREEK - 115
CEDAR CREEK - 25
CHAIN-OF-LAKES - 115
CHERRY CREEK PARK - 49
CHETWOOT - 106
CHEWELAH PARK - 85
CHEWUCH - 126
CHINA HAT - 33
CHOPAKA LAKE - 104
CINDER HILL - 42
CLARK ISLAND STATE PARK - 117
CLEAR CREEK - 46
CLEAR CREEK - 91
CLEAR LAKE SOUTH - 106
CLEARWATER FALLS - 64
CLOUD CAP SADDLE - 53
CLOVER FLATS - 120
CLOVER LEAF - 98
COLD CREEK - 124
COLD SPRINGS - 105
COLD SPRINGS - 121
COLDSPRINGS - 41
COMMONWEALTH - 109

CONTORTA POINT - 24
COOLWATER CAMP - 34
COPPERMINE BOTTOM - 115
CORRAL CREEK - 19
CORRAL CREEK - 82
CORRAL PASS - 94
CORRAL SPRINGS - 22
COTTONWOOD - 94
COTTONWOOD MEADOWS - 42
COUNCIL LAKE - 115
COVER - 67
COW MEADOW - 43
COYOTE - 28
CRANE PRAIRIE - 43
CRAWFISH LAKE - 117
CRESCENT - 56
CREST - 81
CROW CREEK - 107
CRYSTAL COVE - 95
CULTUS CORRAL - 44
CUTTHROAT LAKE - 99
CYPRESS HEAD - 117
CYPRESS ISLAND/PELICAN BEACH - 118
DAIRY POINT - 52
DALEY CREEK - 75
DAVIS LAKE - 81
DE ROUX - 85
DEADHORSE LAKE - 52
DEDUCK SPRINGS - 68
DEEP CREEK - 43
DEEP CREEK - 57
DEEP CREEK - 102
DEEP CREEK - 107
DEER CAMP - 102
DEER CREEK - 65
DEER CREEK SUMMIT - 90
DEER PARK - 114
DEER POINT - 82
DETILLON - 98
DEVILS FLAT - 15
DEVILS HALF ACRE - 35
DEVILS LAKE - 16
DILLON FALLS - 16
DIVIDE WELL - 70
DIXIE - 56
DOE ISLAND STATE PARK - 118
DOG LAKE - 112
DOLLY VARDEN - 46
DOMKE FALLS - 82
DOMKE LAKE - 83
DOSEWALLIPS - 115
DOUGHERTY - 29
DOUGLAS CREEK - 124
DOUGLAS FALLS - 87
DOVE CREEK - 51
DOVRE - 15
DRAGOON CREEK - 120
DRIFT FENCE - 70
DRIFTWOOD - 61

DUCK LAKE - 37
DUMONT CREEK - 67
DUNCAN RESERVOIR - 61
DUNGENESS FORKS - 119
DUSTY SPRING - 68
DUTCH OVEN - 19
EAGLE CREEK - 59
EAGLE FORKS - 59
EAST BAY - 61
EAST CROSSING - 120
EAST LEMOLO - 64
EAST TWIN LAKE - 29
ECHO LAKE - 94
EDGEWATER - 100
EDMISTON - 91
EIGHTMILE CROSSING - 27
ELBE HILLS ORV TRAILHEAD - 92
ELBOW LAKE - 79
ELDERBERRY FLAT - 59
ELDORADO - 71
ELK BEND - 16
ELK CREEK - 56
ELK CREEK - 71
ELK FLATS - 68
ELK LAKE - 27
ELK LAKE - 55
ELKHORN - 58
EMILE SHELTER - 34
ENTERPRISE - 98
ERICKSON'S BAY - 109
ESMERELDA - 92
EVANS CREEK - 94
EVANS CREEK O.R.V. CAMP - 125
EVERGREEN - 40
FAIRVIEW - 38
FAIRVIEW - 63
FALL CREEK - 110
FALL RIVER - 44
FALLS CREEK HORSE CAMP - 82
FAN CREEK - 16
FERRIN - 50
FIFTEEN MILE - 27
FINNER - 102
FIR TREE - 36
FISH LAKE - 37
FISH LAKE - 47
FISH LAKE - 85
FLODELLE CREEK - 87
FOGGY DEW - 123
FOREST BOUNDARY - 113
FOREST CREEK - 73
FORLORN LAKES - 121
FOURTH CREEK - 75
FRAZIER - 54
FRAZIER - 70
FRAZIER TURN AROUND - 30
FRENCH CAMP - 45
FRONA PARK - 49
GIBSON PRAIRIE HORSE CAMP - 53

GODMAN - 91
GOLD DREDGE - 26
GOOSE LAKE - 121
GRAHAM CORRAL - 62
GRAHAM HARBOR CREEK - 83
GRANDVIEW - 42
GRANDY LAKE - 89
GRANITE LAKE - 107
GRASSHOPPER MEADOWS - 103
GREEN MOUNTAIN - 23
GREEN MOUNTAIN HORSE CAMP - 79
GRINDSTONE - 36
GROUSE MOUNTAIN SPRING - 83
HAAG COVE - 100
HALFWAY FLAT - 107
HALFWAY SPRING - 93
HALVERSON - 125
HAM BUNCH CHERRY CREEK - 24
HAMBONE SPRINGS - 30
HANDY SPRING - 83
HANEY MEADOWS - 85
HAPPY CAMP - 52
HARR POINT CAMP - 39
HARRALSON HORSE CAMP - 50
HARTS PASS - 126
HAT POINT - 38
HATCHERY - 83
HEAD OF THE RIVER - 23
HELLER'S BAR - 79
HEMLOCK LAKE - 34
HERMAN CREEK CAMP - 22
HIGH ROCK SPRING - 30
HOBO CAMP - 25
HOH OXBOW - 94
HOLDEN - 83
HOLLYWOOD - 110
HOMESTEAD - 19
HONEYMOON - 126
HOOD RIVER MEADOWS TRAILHEAD - 53
HOPE ISLAND STATE PARK - 118
HORSESHOE LAKE - 30
HORSESHOE LAKE - 116
HOWELL LAKE - 80
HUCKLEBERRY - 58
HUCKLEBERRY - 107
HUELSDONK - 94
HURRICANE CREEK - 40
HUTCHINSON CREEK - 81
ICE CAVE - 122
ICEWATER CREEK - 85
IDLEWILD - 20
ILLAHE - 15
IMNAHA - 20
INDIAN - 68
INDIAN CAMP - 86
INDIAN SPRINGS - 53
INDIAN SPRINGS - 56
INDIGO LAKE - 50
INDIGO SPRINGS - 50

INLET - 27
INLET - 64
IRISH & TAYLOR - 16
ISLAND - 64
ISLAND CAMP - 122
JACK CREEK - 21
JACK LAKE - 21
JACKSON CREEK - 23
JAMES ISLAND - 118
JEAN LAKE - 73
JONES BAY - 99
JONES ISLAND - 118
JONES WELL - 44
JUNIOR POINT - 83
KAMLOOPS ISLAND - 100
KEENES HORSE CAMP - 116
KEEPS MILL - 46
KELSAY VALLEY - 64
KERR - 88
KETTLE RANGE - 117
KETTLE RIVER - 101
KILLEN CREEK - 116
KINGSLEY RESERVOIR - 38
KINNIKINNICK LAURANCE LAKE - 54
KINZEL LAKE - 36
KIRBY CREEK - 51
KLAHANIE - 95
KNEBAL SPRINGS - 28
LADY BUG - 113
LAKE CREEK - 103
LAKE LENORE - 30
LAKE MERRILL - 90
LAKES END - 47
LANE CREEK - 70
LATGAWA COVE CAMP - 39
LAVA CAMP LAKE - 62
LAVA FLOW - 24
LEADER LAKE - 109
LEE THOMAS - 53
LEEP CREEK - 51
LEMOLO TWO FOREBAY - 64
LENA CREEK - 92
LENA LAKE - 92
LESLIE GULCH - 40
LEWIS RIVER - 122
LILLIWAUP - 98
LILLYVILLE - 45
LIMBERLOST - 47
LINNEY CREEK - 36
LION ROCK SPRING - 93
LITTLE BADGER - 69
LITTLE CRANE - 56
LITTLE CULTUS - 16
LITTLE FAN CREEK - 30
LITTLE GOOSE - 122
LITTLE GREIDER LAKE - 99
LITTLE LAVA LAKE - 17
LITTLE TWIN LAKES - 87
LITTLE WENATCHEE FORD - 103

LOFTON RESERVOIR - 19
LONE PINE - 41
LONG CREEK - 71
LONG LAKE - 120
LONG SWAMP - 105
LONGMIRE MEADOW - 107
LOOKOUT SPRINGS - 31
LOST LAKE - 107
LOST LAKE - 112
LOWER ASHLAND LAKE - 97
LOWER CANYON CREEK - 21
LOWER CROSSING - 28
LOWER LAKE - 31
LOWER LEWIS RIVER FALLS - 90
LUCERNE - 84
LUGER SPRING - 69
LUMMI ISLAND - 118
LUNDPARK - 25
LYMAN LAKE - 121
LYNCH CREEK - 52
LYRE RIVER - 114
MAGONE LAKE - 49
MALLARD MARSH - 17
MAMMOTH SPRINGS - 71
MAPLE GROVE - 89
MARBLE CREEK - 105
MARGARET MCKENNY - 110
MATIA ISLAND STATE PARK - 118
McBRIDE - 37
McCUBBINS GULCH - 46
McCULLY FORKS - 65
MCKAY CROSSING - 17
McNAUGHTON SPRING - 57
MEADOW CREEK - 103
MEADOWS - 126
MEDITATION POINT - 36
MELBOURNE - 98
MILE - 17
MILK POND - 108
MILL CREEK - 58
MILLERS LAND - 66
MIMA FALLS TRAILHEAD - 110
MINAM - 48
MINE CREEK - 109
MINERAL - 25
MINERAL PARK - 105
MINNIE PETERSON - 95
MISERY SPRINGS - 113
MITCHELL CREEK - 84
MONTY - 26
MOORE POINT - 84
MORRISON CREEK - 122
MORRISON CREEK HORSE CAMP - 122
MOSIER SPRING - 69
MOSS SPRINGS - 24
MOTTET - 74
MT. HEBO - 37
MT. MOLLY - 110
MT. PILCHUCK REC. AREA - 97

MUD CREEK - 29
MUD CREEK - 43
MUD LAKE - 67
MUD SPRING - 55
MULESHOE - 63
MURRAY - 60
MYRTLE GROVE - 55
MYSTERY - 124
N. FORK ANTHONY CREEK - 37
NAPEEQUA - 103
NATURAL BRIDGE - 58
NE LAKE ELLEN - 101
NESIKA PARK - 23
NICE - 126
NINETEEN MILE - 103
NORTH CATHERINE TRAILHEAD - 71
NORTH COVE - 44
NORTH CREEK - 66
NORTH CREEK - 110
NORTH FORK - 75
NORTH FORK CROSSING - 31
NORTH FORK JOHN DAY - 70
NORTH FORK MALHEUR - 57
NORTH FORK NINE MILE - 105
NORTH FORK SIUSLAW - 33
NORTH GORGE - 101
NORTH TWIN LAKE - 17
OCHOCO - 58
ODESSA - 41
OLALLIE LAKE - 116
OLALLIE MEADOW - 31
OLIVE LAKE - 26
ONION CAMP - 60
OPAL LAKE - 50
ORCAS ISLAND/OBSTRUCTION PASS - 118
ORCAS ISLAND/POINT DOUGHTY - 119
OREGON - 71
OREGON MINE CAMPGROUND - 49
ORIENTAL CREEK - 26
OWHI - 86
PALMER LAKE - 105
PANHANDLE - 124
PANJAB - 113
PANJAB TRAILHEAD - 114
PANSY LAKE - 31
PARISH CABIN - 60
PARK CREEK - 24
PARK CREEK - 89
PATOS ISLAND STATE PARK - 119
PEBBLE FORD - 28
PEGLEG FALLS - 31
PENINSULA - 108
PENIX CANYON - 125
PENLAND LAKE - 38
PHELPS CREEK - 103
PIERRE LAKE - 111
PIETY ISLAND - 27
PIKES CROSSING - 53
PINE NEEDLE - 108

PLEASANT VALLEY - 108
PLUM POINT - 96
POLE PATCH - 116
PONDEROSA - 96
PORTER CREEK - 111
POSEY ISLAND STATE PARK - 119
POST CAMP - 74
PRINCE CREEK - 84
PRINGLE FALLS - 44
QUARTZ MOUNTAIN - 86
R. F. KENNEDY - 80
RAAB - 32
RAINY LAKE - 54
RAMONA TRAILHEAD - 84
RAY COLE - 40
RED BRIDGE - 97
RED MOUNTAIN - 86
RED TOP - 86
REFRIGERATOR HARBOR - 84
RESERVOIR - 44
RHODODENDRON - 90
RHODODENDRON ISLAND - 51
RIMROCK PUBLIC BOAT LANDING - 108
RIVER - 42
RIVER BRIDGE - 58
RIVERFORD - 32
RIVERSIDE - 21
ROADS END - 124
ROCK CREEK - 56
ROCK CREEK - 104
ROCK CREEK - 109
ROCK CREEK CAMP - 125
ROCK LAKES - 110
ROCK SPRINGS - 20
ROCKY LAKE - 88
ROCKY RIDGE - 67
ROME - 20
ROME CAMPGROUND - 60
ROOKE-HIGGINS PARK - 23
ROOSEVELT PARK - 96
ROSLAND - 17
ROUND LAKE - 32
ROUND LAKE - 62
RUFFED GROUSE - 126
RUJADA - 25
SACANDAGA - 51
SADDLE - 123
SADDLE CREEK - 39
SADDLEBAG ISLAND STATE PARK - 119
SAFETY HARBOR - 84
SAN JUAN - 100
SAND SPRINGS - 17
SANDHILL CROSSING - 53
SAUK PARK - 89
SCAPONIA - 60
SCARED MAN - 64
SCATTER CREEK - 86
SCHAEFER CREEK - 104
SCOTTS CAMP - 48

SECRET - 51
SEVEN & ONE-HALF MILE - 22
SEVENMILE MARSH - 41
SHADY - 45
SHADY COVE - 48
SHADY PASS - 93
SHANNON CREEK - 89
SHARPS CREEK - 25
SHEEP BRIDGE - 45
SHEEP CREEK - 101
SHELLROCK CREEK - 32
SHERMAN PASS - 101
SHERMAN VALLEY "Y" - 111
SHINING LAKE - 32
SILVER CREEK MARSH - 61
SILVER KING LAKE - 32
SIXES RIVER - 62
SKAGIT ISLAND - 119
SKOOKUM CREEK - 74
SKOOKUM CREEK - 124
SLIDE CREEK - 57
SLOUGH - 18
SMITH RIVER FALLS - 34
SMOKEY CREEK - 123
SNAG COVE - 101
SNOW CABIN - 120
SNOWSHOE - 20
SODA CREEK - 18
SODA SPRINGS - 104
SODA SPRINGS - 108
SODA SPRINGS - 112
SOUTH - 18
SOUTH - 123
SOUTH CREEK - 124
SOUTH FORK - 21
SOUTH FORK - 72
SOUTH FORK - 108
SOUTH FORK HOH - 95
SOUTH FORK MEADOW - 87
SOUTH NAVARRE - 84
SOUTHWEST OVERFLOW - 66
SPOOL CART - 42
SPRING CREEK - 116
SPRUCE CREEK - 95
SPRUCE GROVE - 93
SPRUCE SPRING - 114
SQUAW LAKE - 56
SQUAW SPRINGS - 69
SQUAW SPRINGS - 69
STARR - 60
STEAMBOAT FALLS - 65
STEVENS CREEK - 72
STOCKADE SPRING - 91
STRAWBERRY - 57
STRAWBERRY/LOON ISLAND - 119
SUGARLOAF - 88
SULPHUR CREEK - 91
SUMMER ISLAND - 101

SUMMIT CREEK - 112
SUMMIT LAKE - 25
SUMMIT LAKE - 36
SUMMIT LAKE - 111
SURVEYOR - 41
SWAMP WELLS HORSE CAMP - 18
SWEDES LANDING - 59
TAHUYA RIVER HORSE CAMP - 80
TAMARACK - 47
TAMARACK SPRING - 87
TEAL - 114
TEANAWAY - 87
TEEPEE - 92
TENAS - 106
TENMILE CREEK - 75
THESEUS CREEK - 104
THIELSEN - 65
THOMPSON RESERVOIR - 61
THREE CREEK - 93
THREE CREEK LAKE - 62
THREE CREEK MEADOW - 62
THREEHORN - 67
TIFFANY SPRINGS - 88
TILLICUM - 123
TILLY JANE - 54
TIME AND A HALF - 42
TIMOTHY SPRING - 69
TIMPANOGAS LAKE - 51
TIPSU TYEE CAMP - 39
TOATS COULEE - 105
TODD LAKE - 18
TOKETEE LAKE - 65
TOLLBRIDGE - 26
TOONERVILLE - 80
TREE PHONES - 121
TROUBLESOME CREEK - 100
TROUT FARM - 57
TROUT LAKE - 102
TUCANNON - 114
TUCKER FLAT - 46
TUCQUALA MEADOWS - 87
TUMALO FALLS - 18
TUNNEL LAUNCH - 59
TWIN FALLS - 123
TWIN FALLS LAKE - 97
TWIN LAKES - 37
TWIN LAKES - 65
TWIN LAKES - 80
TWIN SISTERS PARK - 34
TWIN SPRINGS - 19
TWIN SPRINGS - 32
TWIN SPRINGS - 72
TWO COLOR - 47
TWO PAN - 45
UMATILLA FORKS - 55
UPPER ARM - 27
UPPER ASHLAND LAKE - 97
UPPER CLEARWATER - 115
UPPER END FALL CREEK LAKE - 46

VERMILLION BAR - 52
VIGNE - 29
WAHTUM LAKE - 54
WALKER VALLEY ATV - 81
WALUPT LAKE HORSE CAMP - 112
WELCH CREEK - 27
WELCOME LAKE - 33
WEST CULTUS - 18
WEST TWIN LAKE - 33
WESTERN LAKES - 99
WETMORE - 72
WHISKEY CAMP - 68
WHISPERING PINE - 62
WHITE CREEK - 35
WHITE PASS HORSE CAMP - 113
WHITE PASS LAKE - 112
WHITE RIVER FALLS - 104
WHITE RIVER STATION - 36
WHITECHUCK - 91
WHITEHORSE FALLS - 65
WHITEPINE - 104
WICKIUP - 40
WICKIUP - 79
WICKIUP - 114
WICKIUP BUTTE - 45
WICKY SHELTER - 123
WILD ROSE - 109
WILDWOOD - 58
WILEY FLAT - 58
WILLIAM C. DEARINGER - 91
WILLIAMS CREEK - 38
WILLIAMS LAKE - 88
WILLIAMSON - 46
WILLOUGHBY CREEK - 95
WILLOW CREEK - 43
WINOM CREEK TRAILHEAD - 71
WINSTON CREEK - 82
WOODLAND - 28
WOODLAND - 74
WOODLAND/BRATTON CANYON - 125
WOODLEY - 42
WRANGLE - 39
WY'EAST - 22
WYETH - 45
WYNOOCHEE FALLS - 106
YAHOO LAKE - 95
YELLOW PINE - 72
YELLOWJACKET - 20

GENERAL INDEX

Bicycling - 22, 26, 38, 54, 70.

Boating - 15, 16, 17, 18, 19, 20, 21, 22, 23, 24, 25, 26, 27, 29, 30, 34, 35, 36, 37, 38, 39, 40, 41, 42, 43, 44, 45, 46, 47, 48, 49, 50, 51, 52, 54, 57, 59, 60, 61, 62, 63, 64, 65, 66, 73, 79, 80, 81, 82, 83, 84, 86, 87, 88, 89, 90, 91, 92, 94, 95, 96, 98, 99, 100, 101, 102, 104, 106, 107, 108, 109, 111, 112, 113, 115, 116, 117, 118, 119, 120, 121, 124, 125.

Boat access only - 18, 27, 36, 39, 44, 47, 51, 82, 83, 84, 89, 95, 96, 98, 99, 101, 106, 117, 118, 119, 125.

Boat launch - 15, 18, 20, 22, 23, 27, 29, 34, 35, 38, 40, 41, 42, 44, 46, 48, 49, 50, 52, 59, 60, 61, 62, 63, 65, 66, 79, 80, 81, 86, 87, 88, 90, 92, 94, 96, 98, 100, 101, 102, 104, 109, 111, 112, 115, 116, 117, 120, 121, 124, 125.

Fishing - 15, 16, 17, 18, 19, 20, 21, 22, 23, 24, 25, 26, 27, 28, 29, 30, 31, 32, 33, 34, 35, 36, 37, 38, 39, 40, 41, 42, 43, 44, 45, 46, 47, 48, 49, 50, 51, 52, 53, 54, 55, 56, 57, 58, 59, 60, 61, 62, 63, 64, 65, 66, 67, 68, 69, 70, 71, 72, 73, 74, 75, 79, 80, 81, 82, 83, 84, 85, 86, 87, 88, 89, 90, 91, 92, 93, 94, 95, 96, 97, 98, 99, 100, 101, 102, 103, 104, 105, 106, 107, 108, 109, 110, 111, 112, 113, 114, 115, 116, 117, 118, 119, 120. 121, 122, 123, 124, 125, 126.

Group campsites - 17, 21, 26, 52, 57, 60, 63, 65, 71, 72, 85, 97, 100, 123.

Hike-in access only - 18, 22, 29, 30, 31, 32, 33, 35, 36, 39, 44, 49, 50, 51, 52, 54, 61, 63, 73, 83, 86, 89, 92, 94, 95, 96, 97, 99, 101, 106, 111, 112, 118, 125.

Hiking trails - 15, 16, 18, 19, 20, 21, 22, 23, 24, 25, 26, 27, 29, 30, 31, 32, 33, 34, 35, 36, 37, 38, 39, 40, 41, 42, 43, 44, 45, 46, 47, 49, 50, 51, 52, 53, 54, 55, 56, 57, 58, 60, 61, 62, 63, 64, 65, 66, 67, 68, 69, 70, 71, 72, 74, 75, 79, 80, 81, 83, 84, 85, 86, 87, 89, 90, 91, 92, 93, 94, 95, 97, 98, 99, 100, 101, 102, 103, 104, 105, 106, 107, 108, 109, 110, 111, 112, 113, 114, 115, 116, 117, 118, 119, 120, 121, 122, 123, 124, 125, 126.

Horse facilities - 18, 21, 22, 23, 24, 28, 38, 44, 48, 55, 57, 62, 64, 74, 79, 80, 81, 82, 84, 85, 86, 90, 91, 92, 93, 94, 101, 103, 105, 109, 110, 111, 112, 113, 114, 115, 120, 121, 122, 124, 125.

Lake - 15, 16, 17, 18, 19, 20, 21, 22, 24, 25, 26, 27, 29, 30, 31, 32, 33, 34, 36, 37, 38, 39, 42, 43, 44, 45, 46, 47, 49, 50, 51, 52, 54, 55, 56, 59, 61, 62, 63, 64, 66, 73, 74, 79, 81, 82, 83, 84, 86, 87, 88, 89, 90, 91, 92, 95, 96, 97, 98, 99, 101, 104, 105, 106, 107, 108, 110, 111, 112, 115, 116, 117, 120, 121, 125.

Lake (no motors) - 16, 17, 18, 21, 22, 29, 30, 32, 34, 36, 39, 47, 49, 50, 51, 55, 56, 61, 62, 63, 73, 80, 86, 97, 112, 121.

Oregon cities - 13-75
  Allegheny - 23
  Agness - 15
  Azalea - 15
  Baker City - 15
  Bandon - 15
  Beaver - 15, 16
  Bend - 16, 17, 18, 19
  Blue River - 19
  Bly - 19
  Burns - 20
  Butte Falls - 20, 21
  Camp Sherman - 21, 22
  Cascade Locks - 22
  Cave Junction - 22
  Chemult - 22, 23
  Chiloquin - 23
  Christmas Valley - 23
  Coos Bay - 23
  Coquille - 24
  Cove - 24
  Crescent - 24

Crescent Lake - 24, 25
Culp Creek- 25, 26
Culver - 26
Dale - 26, 27
Detroit - 27
Diamond Lake - 27
Dufur - 27, 28
Elgin - 28
Enterprise - 28, 29
Estacada - 29, 30, 31, 32, 33
Flora - 29
Florence - 33
Fort Rock- 33
Fox - 33
Gardiner - 34
Glide - 34, 35
Gold Beach - 35
Government Camp - 35, 36
Haines - 37
Halfway - 37
Hebo - 37, 38
Heppner - 38
Hood River - 38
Idleyld Park - 38
Imnaha- 38, 39
Jacksonville - 39
John Day - 39, 40
Jordan Valley - 40
Joseph - 40, 41
Kimberly - 41
Klamath Falls - 41
La Grande - 42
Lakeview - 42, 43
LaPine - 43, 44, 45
Lostine - 45, 46
Lowell - 46
Marial - 46
Maupin - 46, 47
McKenzie Bridge - 47
McKinley - 24
Medical Springs- 47, 48
Mehama - 48
Minam - 48
Mitchell - 48
Mt. Vernon- 49
Myrtle Point- 49
Oakridge - 49, 50, 51
Oxbow- 51, 52
Paisley - 52, 53
Parkdale - 53, 54
Paulina - 54, 55
Pendleton - 55
Port Orford - 55
Powers - 55, 56
Prairie City - 56, 57
Prineville - 57, 58
Prospect - 58, 59
Remote - 59

Richland - 59
Rogue River - 59
Rome- 60
Scappoose - 60
Selma - 60
Seneca - 60
Silver Lake - 61
Sisters - 61, 62
Sixes - 62
Spray - 63
Steamboat - 63, 64, 65
Sumpter - 65, 66
Sunriver - 66
Taft - 66
Tiller - 66, 67, 68
Tollgate - 68, 69
Tygh Valley - 69, 70
Ukiah - 70, 71
Union - 71
Unity - 71, 72
Vale - 72
Waldport - 72
Wallowa - 72
Wamic - 73, 74
Westfir - 74
Weston - 74
White City - 74, 75
Whitney- 75
Wimer - 59
Yachats - 75

Scuba diving - 117, 118, 119.

Swimming - 15, 16, 17, 18, 20, 21, 22, 23, 24, 25, 27, 29, 30, 32, 33, 34, 35, 36, 37, 38, 39, 40, 43, 44, 45, 46, 47, 49, 50, 51, 52, 54, 55, 56, 61, 62, 63, 64, 65, 66, 72, 73, 82, 83, 84, 86, 88, 89, 92, 94, 97, 98, 101, 106.107, 108, 111, 112, 113, 115, 116, 121, 122.

Tent camping only - 18, 20, 21, 22, 25, 26, 27, 29, 30, 31, 32, 33, 35, 36, 37, 38, 39, 41, 43, 45, 46, 47, 48, 49, 50, 52, 53, 54, 56, 61, 62, 63, 65, 67, 68, 69, 70, 73, 74, 75, 82, 83, 84, 85, 86, 87, 88, 89, 91, 92, 93, 94, 95, 96, 97, 98, 99, 100, 101, 102, 103, 104, 105, 106, 107, 108, 109, 111, 112, 113, 114, 117, 118, 119, 121, 122, 124, 125, 126.

Trailbikes - 79, 80, 81, 83, 85, 87, 92, 93, 94, 107, 110, 111.

Trailers okay - 15, 16, 17, 18, 19,

20, 21, 22, 23, 24, 25, 26, 27, 28,
29, 30 31, 32, 33, 34, 35, 36, 37,
38, 39, 40, 41, 42, 43, 44, 45, 46,
47, 48, 49, 50, 51, 52, 53, 54, 55,
56, 57, 58, 59, 60, 61, 62, 63, 64,
65, 66, 67, 69, 70, 71, 72, 73, 74,
75, 79, 81, 82, 83, 84, 85, 86, 87,
88, 89, 90, 91, 92, 95, 96, 97, 98,
100, 101, 102, 103, 105, 106, 107,
108, 109, 111, 112, 113, 114, 115,
116, 117, 120, 121, 122, 123, 124,
125, 126.

Washington cities - 79-126
Anacortes - 119
Asotin - 79
Barstow - 79, 80
Belfair - 79
Blind Island - 117
Boyds - 81
Burlington - 81
Carson - 81, 82
Castle Rock - 82
Chelan - 82, 83, 84
Chewelah - 85
Clark Island - 117
Cle Elum - 85, 86, 87
Colville - 87, 88
Conconully - 88
Concrete - 88, 89
Cook - 90
Cougar - 90
Coupeville - 90
Curlew - 90
Cypress Isl. - 117, 118, 119
Darrington - 90, 91
Dayton - 91, 92
Doe Island - 118
Elbe - 92
Eldon - 92
Ellensburg - 92, 93
Entiat - 93
Enumclaw - 94
Forks - 94, 95
Fort Spokane - 95, 96
Glenwood - 121, 122
Goldendale - 96
Grand Coulee - 96
Granite Falls - 96, 97
Guemes Island - 119
Hoodsport - 98
Hope Island - 118
Humptulips - 98
Hunters - 98, 99
Ilwaco - 99
Index - 99, 100
Ione - 100
James Island - 118

Jones Island - 118
Kettle Falls - 100, 101, 102
Leavenworth - 102, 103, 104
Littlerock - 110
Loomis - 104, 105
Loon Island - 119
Lummi island - 118
Marblemount - 105
Matia island - 118
Montesano - 106
Naches - 106, 107, 108, 109
Neah Bay - 109
North Bend - 109
Oakville - 111
Okanogan - 109, 110
Olympia - 110, 111
Orcas Island - 118, 119
Orient - 111
Packwood - 111, 112, 113
Patos Island - 119
Pomeroy - 113, 114
Port Angeles - 114
Porter - 111
Posey Island - 119
Queets - 115
Quilcene - 115
Randle - 115, 116, 117
Republic - 117
Riverside - 117
Rosario - 118
Saddlebag Island - 119
San Juan Island - 119
San Juan Islands - 117-119
Sappho - 94
Sequim - 119, 120
Skagit Island - 119
Spokane - 120
Sucia Island - 119
Tampico - 120, 121
Tonasket - 121
Trout Lake - 121, 122, 123
Twisp - 123, 124
Usk - 124
Vancouver - 124, 125
Washougal - 124
Whidbey Island - 118
White Salmon - 90
Wilbur - 125
Wilkeson - 125
Winthrop - 125, 126
Woodland - 125
Yacolt - 124, 125

Water skiing - 18, 22, 24, 27, 44, 51, 52, 61, 63, 64, 66, 82, 83, 84, 89, 100, 108, 111, 124.

Waterfalls - 64, 65, 82, 87, 90.

141

Wheelchair access - 22, 70, 72, 82, 87, 91, 109, 110, 115, 120, 125.

Wilderness access- 21, 22, 26, 39, 40, 41, 45, 46, 53, 55, 56, 57, 60, 63, 70, 71, 72, 81, 82, 83, 86, 87, 94, 103, 04, 111, 112, 113, 115, 116, 122, 126.

Windsurfing - 24, 96.

ORDER COUPON

Please send:

___UNFORGETTABLE PACIFIC NW CAMPING
VACATIONS - Vol. 1 @ $10.95 ea.   _____

___BEST FREE HISTORIC ATTRACTIONS IN OR/WA;
NORTHWEST FREE - Vol. 1 @ $10.95 ea.   _____

___A CAMPER'S GUIDE TO OR/WA @ $13.95 ea.   _____

___FREE CAMPGROUNDS OF WA /OR @ $8.95 ea.   _____

                                        Shipping   __2.00__

                          TOTAL ENCLOSED   _____

Name _____

Address _____

City/State/Zip Code _____

Send this order coupon to Ki^2 Enterprises, P.O. Box 186, Willamina, Oregon 97396

F95

✂--✂

Please send:

___UNFORGETTABLE PACIFIC NW CAMPING
VACATIONS - Vol. 1 @ $10.95 ea.   _____

___BEST FREE HISTORIC ATTRACTIONS IN OR/WA;
NORTHWEST FREE - Vol. 1 @ $10.95 ea.   _____

___A CAMPER'S GUIDE TO OR/WA @ $13.95 ea.   _____

___FREE CAMPGROUNDS OF WA /OR @ $8.95 ea.   _____

                                        Shipping   __2.00__

                          TOTAL ENCLOSED   _____

Name _____

Address _____

City/State/Zip Code _____

Send this order coupon to Ki^2 Enterprises, P.O. Box 186, Willamina, Oregon 97396

F95

Books by KiKi Canniff

UNFORGETTABLE PACIFIC NW CAMPING VACATIONS; Your guide to Oregon & Washington's most spectacular camping regions. The vacations in this book will take you into some of the region's most beautiful places, tell you where to go fishing, hiking, and see historic sites. Includes both RV and tent campgrounds. *"There's a whole world of natural beauty to explore on the byways and backroads of Oregon and Washington. Nowadays, following those pathways is easier, thanks to the efforts of KiKi Canniff."* **The News-Times.**

NORTHWEST FREE; Volume 1 – THE BEST FREE HISTORIC ATTRACTIONS IN OREGON & WASHINGTON Find out where to see the region's best ghost towns, covered bridges, aging lighthouses, museums, pioneer wagon trails, historic towns, archeological digs, Indian artifact collections, railroad memorabilia and more! *"KiKi Canniff is an expert on freebies"* **Woman's World Magazine.**

A CAMPER'S GUIDE TO OREGON & WASHINGTON; The only complete guide to the region's non-membership RV parks & improved tent campgrounds. The perfect book for campers who want showers, hookups or other civilized facilities. Covers the region's "pay" campgrounds, with information on maximum trailer length, facilities and activities. Easy to follow directions. *This handy guide belongs on every Northwest camper's 'must have' list."* **The Chronicle.**

FREE CAMPGROUNDS OF WASHINGTON & OREGON This book details the two states' 600+ cost-free campgrounds. A terrific book for people who enjoy camping close to nature. *"...very well done, easy to read and to understand ... the cost of this book is saved with the first campground used!"* **This Week Magazine.**

ABOUT THE AUTHOR

KiKi Canniff is a Pacific Northwest writer who specializes in books about Oregon & Washington. She writes a campground column for the Portland Oregonian, and is an avid camper. KiKi also enjoys hiking, travel, history, nature and exploring Pacific Northwest backroads.